QUEEN
of the SKIES

The Inspiring Story of Bessie Coleman

BY BETH POWELL
Contributions by Gigi Coleman and Stephen Walton

QUEEN
of the SKIES

For more information, contact:
Fig Factor Media, LLC | www.figfactormedia.com
Queen B Production, LLC | www.queenbproduction.com
For any inquiries, please email info@queenbproduction.com

Cover Design by DG Marco Alvarez
Cover Layout by LDG Juan Manuel Serna Rosales

Personal photographs in this book are provided with permissions from family, friends, respective entities, or otherwise noted.

Printed in the United States of America

ISBN: 978-1-961600-42-3
Library of Congress Number: 2025901379

Dedication

This book is dedicated to the marvelous and inspiring Bessie Coleman for the impact and the legacy she left and for daring to soar beyond society's limits. This work is for you and all those who take flight because you led the way. To Gigi, whose love for her family and dedication to preserving Bessie's legacy inspires me every day. Your commitment to honoring Bessie's courage and uplifting her story is a gift to all who dream of breaking barriers. Thank you for trusting me to walk this path with you.

To Gigi's mother, Marion Coleman, who first carried the torch of Bessie's legacy with unwavering dedication, ensuring her story was shared with the world. Her relentless commitment and love for family inspired Gigi to continue this journey of honoring Bessie's courage and achievements.

To the future generations of aviators, who now carry the torch of Bessie's legacy with pride and dedication. Bessie's resilience and bravery are your guiding lights, giving you the courage to keep pushing for your dreams. You are our future, and we are counting on you to take flight and soar to great heights.

Table of Contents:

Acknowledgments
By Beth Powell and Gigi Coleman

———

This book would not be possible without the incredible support of many people who have contributed to Bessie Coleman's legacy over the years. We cannot stand here today without acknowledging the village that played a part in preserving and honoring Bessie's impact.

First and foremost, I must acknowledge and thank Gigi Coleman for embarking with me on this great adventure. I feel honored to have had the firsthand experience of connecting with not only you but all of your family. Your dedication to ensuring your Aunt Bessie story lives on is genuinely admirable, and you endlessly inspire me. I could not have done this without you. Thank you to your family for opening your hearts and memories to me. I am eternally grateful.

Additionally, thank you to Stephen Walton, a wonderful friend and collaborator. It has been a pleasure working with you, and our beautiful script that inspired this powerful book. Thank you for your commitment to sharing Bessie's story.

—Beth Powell

———

My heart is full and joyful. I want to express my deepest gratitude to everyone involved in bringing this book to life. As Beth mentioned, it took a village and many years to get us here. I did not do this alone.

Thank you to my family, especially my grandmother, Georgia

Coleman, who was Bessie's baby sister, and my mother, Marion Coleman, who taught me the importance of honoring our heritage. Her endless work with organizations, essay contests, and foundations ensured that Aunt Bessie's name remained known and respected.

To David Quinn, my husband and partner of over twenty-five years, thank you for encouraging me to keep Bessie Coleman's legacy alive after my mother's passing. Your unwavering support from the beginning, from the countless hours spent crafting the script for the Bessie Coleman one-woman show to the Bessie Coleman Aviation All-Stars, has been invaluable in bringing this story to life.

To my twin sons, John Cooper and Jerrard Cooper, who have always proudly upheld the legacy of their grandmother Marion Coleman and their great-aunt Bessie Coleman. Jerrard, an aircraft maintenance technician with an Airframe and Powerplant (A&P) mechanic certification, and John have both embraced their roles in carrying forward our family's story. Thank you for standing by me and keeping our family history alive.

Thank you to my extended family, whose encouragement has been a constant source of strength. Thank you to Vera Jean Ramey, the Eloise Coleman family members, Arthur Freeman, the Nilus Coleman family members, and other Bessie Coleman family members for their unwavering support.

To my lifelong friends and school companions—Antonier Hargrove, Debra Walton, Kim Sackey, Cosandra Ferguson, Artell Cooper, Linda Singleton, Valerie Thompson, Linda Chaney, and Gerri Gibson—thank you for your friendship and encouragement over the years.

To my dear friends who have stood by me and helped bring Bessie's story to life, especially Beth Powell, my partner and co-dreamer on this project; Gloria Blaylock, who served as secretary for our aviation program; the board members and instructors of the Bessie Coleman Aviation All-Stars, which include Stephanie Lewis, Christina Wilson, Derrick Henry, William Cummings, and Dr. William McClinton. I am grateful to Jacqueline Withers, Sheila Chamberlain, Doris Rich, Reeve Lindbergh, William J. Powell, Captain Carole Hopson, Karyn Parsons, Anita Cobbs, Melinda Ragan, Barbara Jackson, Chauncey Spencer, Cassey Grant, Rufus Hunt, Cynthia Anderson, Captain Stan Rasbury, Captain Tony Washington, Captain Antiono Vegas, Captain Lateef Battle, First Officer Michael Calloway, Cherish Black, Civil Air Patrol Coffrey Squadron under Commander Major Richardson, Captain Lou Freeman (first African American pilot at Southwest Airlines), Bernard Young (General Manager of Atlantic Airlines), John Girzadas (President/Manager of B Coleman Aviation), Captain Lester, Gary Percy, Chris Andrew, Ava Ligon, Captain Mika Tang, First Officer Stephanie Grant, Tamora Walls, Natalia Mcalee, Eric Neal, Myiti Sengstacke-Rice, Euzhan Palcy, and Patrick Aglae for their steadfast dedication and support.

A heartfelt thank you to American Airlines for hosting flights to the inaugural All-Black Female Flight in 2022 to celebrate the 100th anniversary of Bessie's pilot license, and for making us their guest for the opening of the reimagined west end galleries at the National Air and Space Museum. We are also grateful to the airline for the "surprise and delight" flight in 2023, which coincided with the launch of the Bessie Coleman Barbie from Mattel, and the special event with the U.S. Mint honoring the launch of the Bessie Coleman quarter. We are also grateful for the airline's donation of 100,000 frequent flyer miles to help students fly to Bessie Coleman All-Star Aviation programs.

I want to acknowledge the many remarkable individuals and organizations who have supported my efforts in honoring the legacy of my Aunt Bessie through our aviation program and my one-woman show. My gratitude goes to Southwest Airlines, American Airlines, United Airlines, and the FAA for organizing tours, field trips, and providing guest speakers for our aviation programs, including Pearlis Johnson, Tony Chu, Georgina Johnson, Tiffany Mathews, Jennifer Curry, James Sulton, Luanne Merrell, Derrick Gaines, and Tyronne Haymore.

Thanks to Republic Airways and the EAA Museum, especially Chris Henry, for enriching our students' experiences. My appreciation to American Duchess, Bessie Coleman Library, Craig Greer and Captain Albert Glenn Luke Weathers Aviation Program, Lewis University, and the invaluable contributions of Sandra Shelton, Paula Kedy Oklahoma Department of Aerospace and Aeronautics, and Lt. General Stacey T. Hawkins at the Tinker Air Force Base Air Show, Afterschool Matters, Gwendolyn Brooks College Prep High School, and the Bessie Coleman Schools in Corvallis, Oregon, Jacksonville, Florida, and Cedar Hill, Texas.

To the historians, associations, and educators who keep Aunt Bessie's history alive, we are grateful to Thelma Rudd, Dr. Nancy Lawrence, Jackie Pilot, Hanna Dixon, and Dorren Branch of the Bessie Coleman Aerospace Legacy, the Chicago Area Pilot Association, the Organization of Black Aerospace Professionals (OBAP), the Chicago Area Pilot Association (CAPA), the Tuskegee Airmen DODO Chapter, Auburn University, Parks St. Louis University, Tuskegee Next, Southern Illinois University, University of Michigan, Evergreen Aviation Space Museum, San Diego Air and Space Museum, Wings Over the Rockies, Delta Flight Museum, Southern Museum of Flight, Palm Springs Air and Museum, Mississippi Aviation Heritage Museum, Women in Aviation, The Ninety-Nines, National WASP WWII Museum, DuSable Museum, the International Women Air & Space Museum in Cleveland, the Smithsonian National Air and Space Museum in Washington, D.C., the National Aviation Hall of Fame, and Sisters of the

QUEEN OF THE SKIES

Skies for their generous donations. Your work ensures Bessie's impact reaches future generations and amplifies her legacy in ways words alone cannot.

For anyone I might have missed, know you are in my mind, and my appreciation is endless. Thank you from the bottom of my heart. Your dedication and shared belief in this project have given me the strength to continue. Together, we honor not only Bessie Coleman but all those who dream of soaring higher.

—**Gigi Coleman**

Foreword
By Gigi Coleman

———

W hen I was a little girl, my grandmother often gave interviews to news reporters about my great-aunt, Bessie Coleman. My grandmother was Georgia Coleman, Bessie's youngest sister out of the thirteen. I would listen intensely to the stories of Bessie's accomplishments, imagining all the amazing daredevil stunts she would perform for shows. I heard how people came from near and far to see the "black lady who flies." It made me immensely proud, and I wished I could have met her.

My mother, Marion Coleman (Georgia's daughter), was the family guardian of Bessie's legacy. She would say that everyone knows Amelia Earhart, but no one knows about Bessie. However, Bessie practically raised my mother when my grandmother, fresh from small-town Waxahachie, was out enjoying city life in Chicago. My mother called my grandmother "Aunt Georgia," which I always found strange. My mother lived in an efficiency apartment with a Murphy wall bed and a shared bathroom near 4750 St. Lawrence in Chicago but traveled everywhere with Bessie. She told me Bessie loved her family and always believed in Almighty God for protection. When my mother relayed the excitement of what Bessie did at her air shows to her cousin, Arthur Freeman, Arthur said nobody believed that a black woman could fly, let alone do stunts.

"Aunt Georgia," as my grandmother was called, and my mother both instilled in me the values of being respectful and kind to others. However, my mother also taught me the importance of a quality education to become self-sufficient. Both women loved me deeply and raised me to be a young lady. I went to all girls catholic schools Aquinas Dominican High School and Mundelein College. I also went to John Robert Power Modeling and Charm school, took ballet lessons in Hyde Park, and had dance lessons downtown with the Joel Hall Dance Company in Chicago.

THE LEGACY KEEPER

I got to know Bessie through my mother. She often spoke of Aunt Bessie's courage, ambition, and determination and how she always wanted to achieve things for the African American people. Bessie traveled abroad to France to pursue her dreams since she couldn't find flight instruction in the U.S. Eventually, she became the first woman African American and Native American to receive her international pilot's license. The news reverberated around the world. She told me Bessie was a gutsy woman who wouldn't take no for an answer. Yet Bessie had a strong feminine side and loved to dress up. When she was not in her flying gear, she was in beautiful dresses and impeccably groomed. However, she happily donned her helmet cap, goggles, long coat, pants, and tall boots when it was time to fly. My mother also told me Bessie was a little fair-skinned and could have passed for white. However, she was proud of her skin color and bi-racial heritage, which included Native American ancestry on her father's side.

As I grew, I saw my mother ensure Bessie's legacy remained in the minds and hearts of people worldwide. She held essay contests at her church, St. Clara Catholic Church in Chicago, to inspire students to explore and learn about Bessie Coleman. She worked with many organizations, like the Bessie Coleman Foundation, founded by Beverly Armstrong, a pilot with the U.S. Air Force, where various women worked in the aviation industry. My mother also started her own foundation, led by Charles Horn from her church and Rufus Hunt, an aviation historian who was part of the Tuskegee Airmen DODO Chapter in Chicago. During her life, she also worked at the Postal Office and in 1995, she petitioned a postal stamp in Bessie's honor after a year's long campaign. My mother also worked with Doris Rich who wrote a book about Bessie. At the DuSable Black History Museum, she worked with Ramon Price (who was the late Harold Washington's brother). They gave her a space and a desk there, and she worked with Margaret Taylor-Burroughs, curator at DuSable, to keep Bessie's legacy alive.

I was still small when pilots began doing annual flyovers of Great Aunt Bessie's grave at Lincoln Cemetery in Alsip, Illinois. The pilots would change yearly, but the formation was always the same. Pilots from the Chicago Area Pilot Association participated, including Darryl Mack, Richard Mack, and William Stewart. Other participating pilots were Keith Reinforce, Rufus Hunt, and Ken Raisper of the Tuskegee Airmen DODO Chapter. The Late Jim Tillman, a CBS2 meteorologist and pilot for American Airlines, also joined. On the day of the flyover, we patiently waited graveside for the roar of the planes overhead. Then they were suddenly there, dropping flowers that fluttered to the ground. My cousins and I would run and pick up all the flowers and place them proudly on Bessie's grave. My mother and granny would sometimes have tears in their eyes.

The flyover became a family event for us. My cousins Vera Jean Ramey, Dean Stallworth, and Arthur Freeman would attend with their children. Yolanda (Yo Yo) rode in the plane one year with Mr. Hunt and dropped the flowers. Vera Jean and Dean were related to Bessie by their grandmother, who was Bessie's sister, Eloise. Arthur's grandmother was Bessie's sister, Nilus. After the flyover, we would go to Vera Jean's house in Harvey for a barbecue. Vera Jean gave us shirts she had made to honor Bessie's family members. Reporters would interview my mother or grandmother on flyover day, which became a completely normal thing to me. By nightfall, I was so tired I would sleep all the way home. I keep the tradition going with my twin boys, John and Jerrard. When they were young, they would come to the grave for the annual commemoration and pick up flowers with their cousins. Now at the commemoration they do a mass balloon release.

THE NEW LEGACY KEEPER

My mother had big dreams of keeping Bessie's memory alive. Many people have written books about her already. The first was Eloise Patterson, Bessie's sister. Charles Lindbergh's daughter, Reeve Lindbergh, published *Nobody Owns the Sky: The Story of "Brave Bessie" Coleman*. She told my mother she felt sorry that her father got all the accolades for his flying and Bessie got nothing. My mother wanted Bessie's story told in school history books. She wanted the world to know about this incredible, beautiful human being who believed in her dreams, persevered, and overcame obstacles to achieve them. She even spoke to a French director and screenwriter before she passed but nothing ever developed during her time. She would have loved to see the work being done now in present time to continue honoring Bessie's life.

When my mother died, I was overcome with grief. I loved her so much, and she was my inspiration. My husband of over twenty-five years, David Quinn, asked me who would keep Bessie's legacy alive. I told him I didn't know. He told me I should since I was Marion's daughter. I accepted the mission but am carrying it out differently than my mother. In 2013, I started a one-woman show where I would dress in character as Bessie and tell her story. I also started an aviation program to inspire youth to think about aviation careers and learn the history of aviation, especially the contributions of minorities. Chauncey Spencer Jr. assisted me with creating the program.

After that I launched, created guidelines in running the program, which encompasses how to operate a flight simulator, field trips to airports and museums, and much more. Our mission is to encourage young people to consider careers in aviation and learn about STEM.

I dedicate this book to my mother, Marion Coleman. I hope she would be pleased with it along with all my other work to keep great aunt's legacy alive. I worked with Jamie Rhee, Chicago Department of Aviation Commissioner, to represent Bessie at various events. We also have a display about Bessie's legacy with artifacts at the United Airlines Terminal at O'Hare International Airport. It was an honor to be at the ribbon-cutting event.

In 2013, Elzie Higginbottom founded the Bessie Coleman Private Airline Company at the Gary/Chicago International Airport, built a ten-million-dollar FBO hangar, and named it after Bessie. In 2015, I did a ten-city tour of some of Bessie's destinations which ended in Rue, Paris, to honor the centennial celebration of her obtaining her license. Some family members attended, and we tried to raise scholarship money for our students to pursue aviation. It was breathtaking to see how the people loved my great auntie and to walk the streets she walked, flew over, and ate at restaurants. I want to thank the people in Abbeville and Rue for all of their assistance in creating a wonderful celebration, especially Francoise Sockeel, Da Jeaneen Johnson-Zanife, Hotel Cauldron, Abbeville flying Club, restaurant Les Aviateurs in Le Crotoy, Johnan Rauch and Karine Bellent, Christine Debouzy, Oliver Sarrazin, Bessie Coleman Film, Mayor of Rue Jacky Thureux, Pamela Edwards, Ashley Thomas, Monica Smith, and all who joined the journey with us.

I applaud the Aircraft Owners and Pilots Association (AOPA)'s You Can Fly Program, which works hard to reach a more diverse audience of future pilots. They include a high school aviation STEM curriculum and provide millions of dollars in scholarships and other initiatives to support and grow the pilot population. Our aviation program has many success stories from graduates like Mya Coley, Ruth Calix, Shawn Littleton, Ronald Gary, Mubahri Aleem, Amiya Davis, Austin Hunter, and Kayla Garrity.

Bessie's contribution to aviation is vast. She has brought diversity and dignity to the industry, and I'm proud to be her great niece and staunch keeper of her legacy. When you read this book, I hope you will also be inspired by her courage and commitment to aviation. Bessie once said, "You've never lived until you've flown." Having flown, she will now live forever in our hearts and on these pages.

Bessie's sisters, Georgia Coleman and Eloise Patterson, along with other family members, including Charles Patterson, Vera Caston, Mr. Allen.

Gigi Coleman, Beth Powell, Sheila Chamberlain, along with Beth's daughter and Gigi's family.

Introduction

By Beth Powell

———

essie Coleman dared to do what others believed was impossible. As the first African American and Native American woman to earn an international pilot's license, she broke boundaries not just in the sky but in the hearts and minds of people around the world. Born in a time and place that offered little opportunity for women, especially women of color, Bessie's pursuit of her dreams took her on an unprecedented journey from rural Texas to the busy streets of Chicago to France, where she found acceptance and encouragement. Her achievements were more than personal victories; they were steps forward for countless individuals inspired by her courage.

This book is not just a biography; it's a family tribute, a legacy passed down from Bessie's sister to her Bessie's niece, Marion Coleman, and now to her grand-niece, Gigi Coleman. Through generations, Bessie's story has become a symbol of resilience, pride, and hope, and it's our privilege to continue sharing it with the world.

My ultimate desire is for more people to know this story and embrace it like I did. It changed me, and I cannot keep this profound impact on myself. I see myself in Bessie as a woman of color, a pilot, a lover of family, and a breaker of barriers. Perhaps that's why I am so compelled to tell her story. Although I didn't learn about Bessie's story until later in life and into my career, it's as if I knew her all my life. It has been a privilege to connect with her family and learn the details and stories passed down about her life. Hearing the memories and recollections and getting an inside look into the Coleman family, I feel like Bessie is my family, too.

When I began my production company, Queen B Production, I wanted to share the power of storytelling with purpose. Especially stories that bring people together. Bessie's story does that and more. It has increased awareness of Bessie's achievements and united people and organizations, but most importantly, it has brought hope. Hope for continuous change, representation, and acceptance in the aviation field. I see a future where access to positions in aviation and aviation leadership is open to all, based on our qualifications and merits, not just for the selected few regardless of sex, race, or gender. This is Bessie's legacy, alive and well, and I am excited to see where it goes next.

I also want to honor the many supporters and allies who have contributed to bringing Bessie Coleman's story to light in their own ways. Through factual accounts and creative re-imaginings, we share a common mission of showcasing resilience, determination, and empowerment. Special recognition goes to those whose works have paved the way for this book—each has enriched Bessie's legacy with their dedication and imagination. Thanks to these efforts and allyship, we can build upon a foundation of inspiration and historic preservation. I hope that future generations will have even more insights, stories, and archives to explore so Bessie's legacy may continue to inspire for years to come.

May this book inspire you to soar beyond boundaries and carry forward her message: that the sky truly has no limit.

PART 1

A Little Girl with a Dream

CHAPTER ONE

Home and Heart

———

The hot Texas sun bore down on the dusty yard outside the small Waxahachie, Texas, Baptist church in 1904. It cast long shadows over the rugged wagon waiting by the worn wooden steps. George Coleman, a tall, broad-shouldered, Native American man with a face that showed his Choctaw heritage, walked with a determined step beside Reverend Henry Miller. The preacher, small and wiry with a shock of white thinning hair, kept pace. Around the two men, the churchgoers, dressed in their finest frills and broadcloth, spilled into the dirt street. The children, released from their obligation to sit still and be quiet, left the church at a full trot, kicking up dust as they looked around for their friends. As the adults lingered with each other exchanging pleasantries, the boys seized the opportunity to start a game of tag while the girls gathered to admire each other's Sunday dresses.

Reverend's gaze was steady on George's troubled face between greetings to his congregants. As they got closer to the Coleman family wagon, the two men could speak more privately. Susan Coleman, George's wife, was already perched on the wagon's front seat, her face set with a quiet patience from long years of scraping by. Her eyes, sharp as a hawk's, scanned the yard, settling on her children scattered around, chattering with friends.

"Bessie Coleman! Walter! Get over here, we're leaving!"

Eight-year-old Bessie shot a glance at her twelve-year-old brother, Walter, before they took off running, bare feet stirring up small clouds of dust. Their siblings, Isaiah and Georgia, yelled encouragement from the back of the wagon where they were already seated. Walter and Bessie reached the wagon as her father and Reverend Miller approached. Walter climbed into the wagon box first, then helped Bessie up. She listened closely and caught the tail end of the men's conversation as Walter scrambled into the back of the wagon with the other Coleman kids.

"The Lord will provide, no matter what you choose," the Reverend said. He smiled at Susan before turning his attention back to her husband. "But you're right, George. You're no good to your family dead." George nodded, a faint smile cracking his otherwise grim expression. "Thank you, Reverend. Sometimes, it's more than I can stand. Lord knows it's a messed-up world."

"It is that." Reverend Miller patted George's arm. "'Member, the Lord is always with you, no matter your path."

George mounted the front seat beside Susan and shook the reins. The wagon creaked and rocked as George urged the mule forward, and the family set off down the rutted road toward home. The family passed the modest, bare wood-sided buildings of Waxahachie's downtown with their wide porches shaded by awnings and their goods attractively displayed behind their large picture windows. On the rough-hewn, wood-planked sidewalks outside the stores, the churchgoers who were lucky enough to travel to church on foot marched alongside the wagon until the mule Charlie overtook them. As the wagon passed the candy store, the Coleman children murmured excitedly at the large lollipops and jars of penny candy displayed in the window. Bessie, however, was more interested in her parents' conversation.

Susan glanced sideways at George, catching his expression.

"You expected a straight-up answer from the Reverend?" she asked dryly, her voice a mix of teasing and resignation.

George shook his head, the corners of his mouth lifting just a fraction. "Expect not. Would be nice, though."

Behind them, Bessie sat cross-legged in the wagon bed, her eyes closed as she leaned back, letting the sun warm her face. The town seemed to fade away as they started down a lonely, grass-lined road to their family homestead. She was listening intently, picking up every word from her parents' hushed voices. Walter sat nearby. He hunched his shoulders as if he felt the weight of what lay unspoken between their parents.

Susan sighed. She fixed her gaze on the road ahead. "We gonna have to decide, like he said. You know I love you more than anything in this world."

George's voice softened. "I know that. Only thing more precious to the both of us is the kids here."

Susan's voice dropped to a whisper, thick with worry. "My heart'd break if something happened to you. It'd be killing all of us."

"So you're saying I need to go?" His words came out like a challenge, tinged with an unspoken plea for her to say no.

She hesitated before replying. "I'm sayin' we got a house and land here, with school and work. Our house, our land. We ain't gonna have none of that if we ran off to the Territories with you."

Bessie cracked her eyes open, glancing at Walter. He met her gaze, his face tense, showing he'd been listening too. She bit her lip, turning her face away to hide the sting of tears welling up.

George gritted his teeth. "Ain't right a man works for all this and gets run off."

Susan sighed again, and her voice was quiet but unyielding.

"You wouldn't be running from us, though. Maybe you get set up out there, maybe not. Couldn't take it if you're not in this world." She nodded to the children in the back. "Don't expect they'd be too happy either if you ain't breathing."

Bessie shut her eyes tightly, feeling a tear slip free. They rode the rest of the way in silence until the small Coleman house came into view. It was a rough-hewn structure painted white, surrounded by a sparse acre of land with a garden patch and a weathered shed. George pulled the reins, bringing the wagon to a halt.

"Okay, all you kids get to it," George ordered, the weight in his voice barely hidden. "Walter, you and Isaiah tie Charlie out in the grass once you get'm unhitched." Susan chimed in the duty roster. "Georgia, go fetch some water. Bessie, light up the stove."

As ten-year-old Isaiah walked Charlie towards the shed, the girls hurried into the house. Georgia grabbed a bucket and headed for the water pump as Bessie prepared the wood stove for the evening meal. As she worked, Katos, the gray barn cat, slinked through the open door and rubbed up against her legs. She scooped him up, burying her face in his soft fur for comfort before setting him back down. Meanwhile, George and Susan walked towards the house together as Susan's gaze fell onto the endless cotton fields stretching into the distance.

"We ain't picking for another few months," she said quietly, her eyes on the far-off line of trees. "And it's gonna be cold up there by then. Might want to light out sooner 'n later."

George's shoulders slumped, then straightened, a decision settling over him like a heavy coat. He met her gaze, nodding slowly. "Guess you're right. Ain't much more I can do 'round here…'cept maybe get killed."

A few mornings later, the rooster crowed as usual, announcing the first light. In the dim kitchen, Susan bent over the stove, lighting an oil lamp with a thin stick to start breakfast. Walter eased past her, heading toward the outhouse, rubbing the sleep from his eyes.

In the small sleeping room, Katos lay curled on Bessie's pillow, his ears flicking up as he sensed her stirring. Bessie sat up, reached over, and nudged her sister.

"Come on, Georgia. We got school."

Georgia groaned, pulling the blanket tighter. "Don't wanna."

"You stick 'round here, Momma gonna work you hard. Best get up. You're gonna miss school soon enough."

Bessie pulled a protesting Georgia to her feet, and they hurriedly dressed for the new day. In the kitchen, Georgia laid out the bowls as Susan filled each with hominy grits, adding a small piece of ham to each. Nine pairs of hands reached eagerly for their breakfast before they settled around the wooden table.

"Georgia, you wanna say grace?" Susan said.

Georgia folded her hands, bowing her head. "Dear Jesus, we thank you for our food and family. Thank you for the love you share and the love of our family."

After finishing breakfast, the family stacked their bowls in the basin.

"Children, you all know what ya got to do. Best get to it," Susan said, helping hurry her brood out the door.

Outside, the morning sun rose, casting a warm, hazy light over the winding dirt road. Bessie's bare feet moved steadily over the rough path. Georgia, Walter, and Isaiah trudged beside her. The four of them made this walk every school day, four long miles each way, through town and past the sagging buildings that marked the dusty heart of Waxahachie.

In the town square, Bessie's eyes flickered over a solemn sight: a thick oak tree with a faded, frayed rope dangling ominously from one of its low branches. Walter glanced at her, and she could tell he saw it too. It was the silent remnant of old hatred that hadn't faded.

They reached the whitewashed schoolhouse and joined their respective lines—the boys and girls—before filing into the classroom and finding their respective desks according to grade. Mrs. Braden, a petite woman with boundless energy, greeted each child with a warm smile as they entered. Her voice was gentle but firm as she raised a hand, signaling the start of the day.

"Thank you, children. Settle down now, if you please. We start, as always, with a prayer. Iris Johnson, would you do us the honors this morning?"

She handed Iris Johnson a printed page. Iris, tall for her twelve years, stood by her desk next to Bessie, clutching the paper like a lifeline. Her hands shook slightly as she began to read in a soft voice.

"Thank you, God, for all the things you've made our world to be. Thank You, God, for all the people you've placed around us." Her voice grew steadier as she continued. "Thank you for the gifts you send us every day, every meal or game we play. Thank you, God, for caring for us; we know you always see our every worry, care, and fear. Our laughter and our sadness."

Iris paused and looked around at the class before continuing. There was a mix of engagement and disinterest. "Thank you, Lord, that you're our friend. You delight in all we do, especially when you hear our prayers, and we give thanks to you."

Iris sat down with a sigh of relief,, and Mrs. Braden gave her a gentle nod before addressing the room.

"Okay, children, turn to your lesson books where you left off. I'll come around if you have questions."

Her eyes rested on Bessie. "Bessie, honey, I need you to help the third graders with their 'rithmatic. They're starting on the times tables."

Bessie rose and moved to the row of younger children at the front, each clutching a small slate and piece of chalk. Mrs. Braden knew Bessie enjoyed teaching and had a knack for it, too. Standing beside the blackboard, Bessie smiled at the handful of third graders.

"Alright, let's start. It's pretty easy once you see it, but sometimes it can take a little while. So ask if you don't understand."

She wrote a "1" on the board, underlining it. "Okay, we're starting with the 'Ones.' One times any number is just itself. 'X' means 'times,' so one times one is… Joshua?"

Joshua, a small boy with wide eyes and clean but well-mended clothes, answered cautiously.

"One?"

"That's right. Now, two times one is?"

"Two!" he replied, his face lighting up.

Bessie's laughter mixed with the children's murmurs as they echoed the answers, each gaining confidence as they moved up through the numbers. She liked math. All the outcomes were predictable and consistent.

The day passed quickly, and the Coleman children started home as the sun made its way west.. As they passed through town, Bessie and Walter lingered behind as the others walked ahead, their gazes fixed on the worn, silent rope swaying in the old oak tree.

"You think that's what Daddy was talkin' about?" Walter asked in a hushed tone.

Bessie nodded. Her eyes grew dark with understanding. "You know it is."

"That's from a while ago—couple years, ain't it?"

"Yeah. But ain't nothing changed." Bessie's voice held a hard edge. "Daddy was right to get to the Territories. And we gotta be careful, too."

Bessie looked around the town. She saw two black women on the sidewalk up ahead lower their heads and reflexively step off the narrow sidewalk as two white women approached. They then returned to the path, not breaking stride, as if it were second nature. Bessie watched the scene with narrowed eyes, taking in the "No Colored" sign in the dry goods store window nearby.

Catching her expression, Walter muttered, "I hear up north that don't happen. Don't have to step out of nobody's way 'cept to keep from walkin' into 'em."

"Up north, huh?" Bessie's tone was curious, her eyes turning thoughtful.

"Yeah. Detroit, Chicago. I figure once I finish school, I'm headin' that way, long as Mama and you all gonna be alright."

The children fell silent for a moment, each lost in their thoughts. Then Walter glanced at her, his tone laced with a challenge.

"What you gonna do when you finish school, huh? Stick around here doing washin' and pickin' cotton?"

Bessie's brow furrowed, and she shook her head. "I don't wanna do that. Ain't nothing wrong with it, but I'd like to do more. Daddy said I can do anything I put my mind to."

Walter raised an eyebrow, curious. "Like what?"

"Like goin' up to C.A.N.U. in Oklahoma."

He rolled his eyes. "Colored Ag and Normal University? And what you gonna study there? How to wash clothes? Be a proper 'Domestic'? Maybe become a teacher…"

Her shoulders slumped slightly, but she kept walking, her gaze fixed ahead.

Walter's voice softened, almost as if he regretted his teasing. "That's all they think people like us can do. Used to whip us just for learnin' to read. Guess that's 'progress.'"

Bessie took a deep breath. "Being a teacher ain't bad. I already help Mrs. Braden, and I like it."

Walter shot her a skeptical look. "You think you're gonna like it day after day?"

She glanced at him, a teasing light in her eyes. "Not if I get students as dumb as you."

Walter laughed, giving her a light shove. "I know you, sis. You're gonna do things in this world. And ironing or tapping on a chalkboard all day ain't it."

His words settled over her, and for the first time in a while, Bessie allowed herself to imagine something bigger, a future beyond Waxahachie. She squared her shoulders, picking up her pace to catch up with the others, her heart lifting with a glimmer of hope.

****

Laundry day was sunny and breezy. The Coleman farm undulated with the sight of the white sheets and shirts on the line, gracefully furling back and forth against the cloudless, bright blue sky. Bessie hung damp sheets on the line, watching as it caught the wind, billowing like a sail. Beside her, seven-year-old Elois folded the dry ones into a wicker basket. Along the back of the house, large tubs of soapy fresh water stood ready with washboards to receive the family's clothes. The heavily soiled ones were treated to a warm bath in a vat heated underneath by a small fire.

Walter appeared. His brow was already glistening with sweat as he poured water from a bucket into the steaming vat and stirred the swirl of colored clothes in it with a wooden paddle. Susan and Elois scrubbed the clothes on worn washboards, their hands moving in a steady rhythm, the sound of sloshing filling the air.

"Momma, we gotta finish all this today?" Walter asked, his tone halfway between a complaint and a plea.

Susan didn't look up as she scrubbed, her voice resolute. "The work's here now. When you think it's a good time to do it?"

Walter hesitated, glancing around at the growing piles of clothes. "Just seems there's a lot," he muttered.

At that moment, Katos trotted by, a dead mouse hanging from its mouth.

"Don't work, ya don't eat," she said, gesturing toward the cat. "Even the damn cat's got that figured out. We got lots of mouths to feed." She paused, casting a sidelong glance at Bessie. "An' Bessie still wants to go off to the C.A.N.U."

Bessie had shared her dream with her mother, even knowing as she did that it probably wouldn't come true. Walter leaned on his paddle, his eyes shifting to his sister. "You still fixin' to run up there after you finish school?"

Bessie nodded, a spark of determination in her eyes. "You know I am. That's why I'm bringin' in the extra work. What we don't use is goin' into the bank."

Walter grinned, raising an eyebrow. "So, do I get a share of this?"

Susan shook her head, smirking. "You get your share to eat an' clothes on your back, an' tomorrow you get gloves for pickin', less'n you don't think you'll need 'em."

"Yes, ma'am," he replied, though the smile had faded from his face. "Just hope this'll be the last time pickin'," he muttered under his breath.

"We get this crop in an' Mr. Johanson pays us, then you can up and scoot off to Chicago or wherever you please," Susan said. "Right now, you're part of this family. There's work to do."

The Old Texas Theater in Downtown Waxahachie, TX.

CHAPTER TWO

Out of the Fields

———

M r. Johanson, a weather-beaten farmer in his fifties, eased his horse-drawn wagon to a halt at the edge of the cotton field. Rows of cotton stretched out before them, white dots against the cloudless blue morning sky. The Coleman family sat on the wagon bed, gazing at the endless, sea of ripe white cotton plants, their branches heavy with fluffy bolls awaiting the harvest.

"Whoa up there, Ruffy. Whoa," Johanson murmured, firmly pulling on the reins. "Okay, folks, end of the line."

Susan lifted her hat slightly, giving Johanson a steady look. "So's we're clear. Same as last year, fifty-fifty."

The Coleman family, all dressed in long sleeves and broad hats, exited the wagon and began to unload their harvesting bags and water barrel.

"Same as last year and the year before," Johanson replied with a nod, tipping his hat. "Fifty-fifty."

Susan stepped off the wagon and reached into a cloth sack to hand out worn gloves to her children. Johanson released the wagon's brake and shook the reins, preparing to leave.

"Hup, Ruffy, hup."

The horse clopped forward, and the wagon creaked as it turned back onto the dirt road, leaving the Coleman family alone at the edge of the vast cotton field.

Susan squared her shoulders. "Let's get to it, children."

They moved into the field, each Coleman family member settling into a row and pulling their bags behind them. They bent low, reaching into the cotton plants, plucking the bolls with steady hands, and placing them into the harvest bags. The rhythm was quick and steady—each boll carefully twisted off and tucked away.

The family's initial chatter fell silent as the sun climbed higher and beat down on them mercilessly. Sweat dripped down their faces as they picked, and each pull, each twist, and each drop of cotton into their bags felt like a drop in an endless ocean. The morning passed, and the field stretched on, unyielding.

At noon, they paused to eat and drink water from the small barrel, resting briefly under the shade of a tree. Susan surveyed the field wearily. They had only harvested a quarter of it.

Walter's eyes followed his mother's and came to the same conclusion. "Guess we'll be here tomorrow too," Walter muttered, earning a laugh from Bessie as she took a swig of water.

By late afternoon, bags bulging with cotton lined the edge of the field, waiting for Johanson's return. Soon enough, they heard the creak of the wagon, and the old horse, Ruffy, ambled back toward them, pulling the wagon for the day's load.

"That's some fine work," Johanson said as he approached, scanning the bags. "'Magine you'll be done with this one tomorrow."

Susan nodded, giving a slight nod. "Reckon so. We still got them other two to do. It'll be Friday we're done."

"Looks like it," he said, glancing around. "Ya'll got whatcha need?"

"I 'xpect so," she replied, then turned to the kids. "Come on now, let's get this weighed 'n on the wagon. Bessie, get over there 'n write it down."

CHAPTER TWO: OUT OF THE FIELDS

Bessie moved over to the scale, notepad in hand, carefully noting each bag's weight. Johanson watched her with a hint of amusement.

"What's the matter, Miss Susan?" he asked, an eyebrow raised. "Don't trust me?"

Susan's eyes met his cooly. "I trust in the Lord Jesus, Mr. Johanson. Everyone else gonna have to make an account'n."

With that, she turned back to the weighing, her attention unwavering. The last cotton was loaded, spilling from the sack to the wagon bed, overflowing with the family's hard work. As Johanson and Ruffy plodded off, the Colemans put their bags back on, moving back into the field with a resigned determination.

The next day, the family returned to repeat the process. As the children walked further out into the field, past yesterday's work and to the plants that held the tantalizing fluffy white bolls, Bessie paused. As she straightened up and stretched out her body, which was stiff from the work the previous day, her eyes drifted skyward. Overhead, a lone hawk glided effortlessly in the warm air currents, wings spread majestically. For a moment, Bessie felt a strange sense of peace watching it, a calmness among her tired limbs and sore fingers. She couldn't resist stretching her arms out to the sides, feeling the breeze against her skin as she spun herself around slowly, eyes on the hawk, trying to imagine what it felt like to fly like him, free and unbound. It must be a magical feeling, Bessie thought.

But her smile faltered as she watched the hawk suddenly tuck in its wings, diving toward a dove below. It snatched the smaller bird in its claws and carried it to the ground. Bessie winced. Her momentary freedom was dashed by the sharp reality of the hawk's nature.

Soon, the sun was low on the horizon, and the air was thick with the heat of a day's labor. Most of the plants around them were stripped bare of their bolls. Bessie, her bag three-quarters full, stumbled slightly under its weight as she moved forward.

"Come on, Bess, you're a'right. One foot in front of t'other," she heard Walter call out, his voice soft but encouraging.

Bessie caught herself, nodding with a small, grateful smile. She straightened up and reached for another boll, her hands moving with determination.

"Gett'n there, Walter," she murmured. "Wherever 'there's' gonna be."

And, just for a moment, with the last of the sun casting its golden light across the field, she could almost feel that freedom again.

The day's picking and the ones ahead produced a tidy sum for the family. Bessie was motivated to attend CANU in the fall. She took in as much extra laundry and ironing as she could, hurrying home from school to work long hours into the evening to make additional dollars for tuition. When she sent in a letter of application and received one in reply, she was overjoyed.

"Mama! I'm in! I'm in!"

Susan smiled a worried, small smile, but her eyes twinkled with delight as she folded Bessie into her arms. She had no idea what the future held for her little girl, but she would soon find out.

Finally, the day arrived. The dawn broke icy and brittle over Waxahachie as Charlie drove the Coleman family's wagon along the frozen road. Wheels crunched through thin ice, puddles fracturing under the weight. Wrapped in heavy coats and sweaters, Susan, Bessie, and Walter dismounted and approached the train station, bracing against the cold.

The small, dimly lit office of the station master was warmed only by a small potbelly stove. The station master, an older, thin white man with a cap pulled low over his gray hair, looked up as they approached his window. "Morning, ladies. How may I help you?" His voice was polite but perfunctory.

Bessie held out three crumpled bills, her hand steady but betraying the effort behind saving every dollar. "One ticket to Oklahoma City, continuing on to Guthrie, please, sir."

The station master squinted, consulting a well-worn rate schedule on the wall. "Oklahoma City, then Guthrie... That'd be three dollars even."

Taking the money, he nodded knowingly, sensing the struggle behind every hard-earned cent. He slid the ticket across to Bessie with a quiet, "Last two coaches for you."

Outside, Walter handed two rough, well-worn suitcases to the black porter on the train. A tearful Susan and Bessie embraced tightly, as if the hug could somehow span the miles they'd soon be apart. Bessie tore herself from her mother to give Walter an equally significant hug. Her eyes were filled with tears now.

"'Member, Bessie. You're gonna do things in this world," he reminded her.

Bessie climbed aboard the train hesitantly, looking over her shoulder as she left her old world behind. She made her way past the white faces in the front of the train, whisking away the tears from her eyes. The back of the coach was filled with serious, yet somehow friendlier, dark faces, many in family groups. Bessie slid into the smooth, worn leather seat behind a mother and her baby and gazed out the window. She saw Walter and her mother climbing into the wagon to head home. The train lurched forward, and Bessie was on her way.

Almost instinctively, she rose out of a dead sleep many hours later, somehow feeling the landscape had changed. Bessie looked out the window and beheld snow-dusted grassy areas whipping by her window. Then, suddenly, she saw signs of a small town covered in a thin frost. It was Langston, Oklahoma.

The Reconstruction-era town was nestled amid the frozen rolling prairie. From her seat, Bessie could see the town's wooden-frame houses and narrow dirt streets with many of the same shops Waxahachie had, like the general store, the barber, and the blacksmith. Yet this town had a different energy and was populated by people who looked just like the travelers. It was sprucer, with storefronts standing shoulder to shoulder, freshly painted in muted shades of white, brown, or green with seasonal decorations. Shoppers bundled up in scarves, hats, and woolen coats, moved among them busily. Bessie imagined them doing their Thanksgiving shopping early.

As the train slowed, she saw the omnibus wagon trundling down the main street, pulled by a team of determined-looking brown horses in modest leather harnesses with polished brass fittings. They pulled the tall, spoked wheels forcefully over the rutted, semi-frozen roads, knowing they could rest a bit once they reached the train passengers. Compared to the transportation options in Waxahachie, Bessie thought the omnibus looked quite luxurious. The wood sides were painted dark green and reinforced with attractive metal fittings that added an air of dignity. The wheels had iron rims to endure the town's rough cobblestone or dirt roads while transporting multiple passengers. The wagon had a flat roof, and the passengers boarded with the aid of a fold-out stair at the opening to the omnibus. The driver collected their suitcases and stored them overhead as the passengers took their place on the wooden benches lining the sides of the wagon.

Bessie took her place in the rear between a couple traveling with a child and an older woman. Soon, the conductor passed by, collecting fare from all the passengers. Bessie handed him a coin and sunk back in her seat. The sliding curtains over the windows did not keep out the chill of the outside air, but Bessie was almost too excited to feel it as she peered out at her new home. Many other passengers, who were also first-time visitors to the town, did the same.

"They got a pharmacy," a woman pointed, her voice awed.

Another man joined in, "Library too. And everyone is of the race."

"Ain't never seen nothing like this in my life," a second man muttered.

The omnibus clattered to a stop in front of an impressive three-story brick building which was the university's main hall. It was flanked by two dormitories, one each for men and women. Standing at the foot of the steps of the hall's entrance were Doris Fairday, a prim-looking, forty-six-year-old woman, and Danial Clayman, a fifty-one-year-old man with a white beard, graying hair, and kind eyes. Both administrators were sharply dressed.

"Welcome, students, welcome one and all," Doris called out, her voice warm and encouraging.

Danial's comments were more perfunctory. "Please, form lines. Ladies to my left, gentlemen to my right. We have some tasks to accomplish, and then you'll be settling in."

Doris, with a brisk smile, gestured to the main hall doors. "Find your papers and follow us. Your luggage will be waiting for you as you exit." Bessie clutched her belongings and joined the line, stepping eagerly into the bustling energy of her new school.

The main hall was modestly impressive, with dark woodwork and plenty of natural light. Inside, students in blue uniforms sat at tables along the entryway, ready to check in the new arrivals. Processed students, holding freshly issued uniforms, gathered nearby in a queue.

Danial pointed down the hallway and announced, "Please see the finance office folks after you register."

Doris nodded. "Ladies and gentlemen, once in your dorm, please try on your uniforms. We pride ourselves on a crisp look here," she said. "If you find the fit inadequate, return here, and we will see it put right."

Bessie smiled as one of the students handed her a new uniform that looked her size. She couldn't wait to try it on. When she got to her assigned dorm room, she opened the door and was surprised to be immediately followed inside the door by a plump, short girl about her age.

"Oh....hi," Bessie said.

"You must be Bessie," the girl said. "You're Bessie, right?"

Bessie nodded slowly. "They told me my roommate was Bessie. I'm Francine," she said, hurrying past Bessie into the room. "We're roommates."

Bessie beheld the sun streaming through a small window, lighting the spartan yet adequately furnished dorm room. She noticed Francine was carrying her freshly issued uniform, too. Francine looked around, hesitant to pick a side of the room with a bed and dresser.

Bessie, in her easygoing way, smiled. "Your choice of bed. Won't make a difference to me."

Francine glanced around, looking both excited and shy. "Me neither. Never had a bed to myself."

Laughing, Bessie replied, "Me neither! I've got lots of brothers and sisters, too!"

Francine's smile grew. "Yeah, we's kinda crowded too."

Bessie slept deeply that night, even though she was excited to wake up and start her studies. During her first class, Dr. Louis Snead, a black man of fifty with a refined air and a well-tailored suit, stood in front of his students with a commanding presence. His gaze swept over the students intently as if memorizing their faces in one pass.

"Good morning, class. Welcome." He paused, letting his words sink in. "You may have noticed that I said good morning, not g'morn'n. In this class, we will practice elocution."

The students listened, captivated by his calm authority.

"We come from different parts of the country," he continued, nodding toward the American flag in the corner of the room. "Where we were raised and with whom affects our speech. But the country we come from—the United States of America—is a child among nations. If the race is to take its rightful place, we must communicate effectively."

The students exchanged thoughtful glances as his words registered.

"Make no mistake," Dr. Snead declared, his voice resonating. "You are as smart as anyone you will meet. Your ideas are just as brilliant. But you will be judged within heartbeats if your speech is different or deficient." Gesturing toward the classroom's globe, he added, "Many of you will travel this world, and your ability to communicate will be key to your success."

Dr. Snead was impressive, but Bessie enjoyed rhetoric class and the teacher, Paralee Lucas, even more. She was a petite woman who radiated authority.

"When people interact, differing opinions will arise," she began, her voice warm and unhurried, "whether it's on matters of politics—or simply what to cook for dinner." The students replied with a smattering of laughter.

"The purpose of this class," she continued, "is to teach you how to organize your thoughts and present them effectively, even to the opposition." She let her gaze linger on several students who seemed to find what she was saying amusing.

"Some of you may be surprised to see a woman teaching this class," she observed, "but in your life's experience, you know there's no one better to teach argument than a woman."

Several of the male students rolled their eyes playfully.

"Argument, properly pursued," she emphasized, "is the statement of well-thought-out ideas, not a blurting out of emotion." She looked pointedly at Bessie and Francine, two of the few women in the classroom.

"Let's open our texts. You'll see that much of our argument structure has roots in the Greeks and Romans…"

Before Bessie knew it, it was Christmas time. She strolled down the decorated hallway, Christmas trimmings brightening the wood-paneled walls. She carried herself with a mixture of purpose and reluctance, finally stopping at the door of President Inman Page's office.

Inside, President Page sat behind a modest but imposing desk, surrounded by books and polished wood shelves. He looked up as Bessie entered, his demeanor kind but assessing.

"So, what brings you here today?" His tone was calm, but his expression was probing.

Bessie hesitated, shifting in her seat. "Well, sir… must let you know I'm leaving school at the end of the semester."

President Page's eyebrows lifted slightly, surprised. "And pray tell, child, what would be the reason? Your grades have been outstanding."

Bessie swallowed, finding her words carefully. "It's not the academics. I love everything about being here. But honestly, it comes down to money, sir."

The president folded his hands, leaning forward. "So, what have you in mind, young lady?"

Looking down briefly, Bessie answered, "Looks like I'll be

heading home. Momma and the family need me. This school opened my eyes to the world. I doubt I'll be staying in Texas too long."

He regarded her with sympathy and understanding. "Ambition. There's nothing wrong with that." He smiled warmly. "And if you decide to return, you're more than welcome."

"Thank you, sir." Bessie's voice was filled with gratitude and a glimmer of determination. "There's just so much of this big world. I don't know where I'll go... but I'm ready to find out."

****

As hard as it was to leave CANU, Bessie knew it was the right thing to do. Susan was now alone. George had left for the Oklahoma territories where he would be safe from the hatred and violence towards his race that had settled over Texas. As a Native American, he could live with respect as a citizen in the Oklahoma Indian Territory. Susan worked as a cook and housekeeper for a white couple and Bessie was needed at home to fill in for her mother and care for her younger siblings.

Back home, in the familiar, well-worn kitchen, stacks of laundry baskets bordered the room like tiny fortresses of fabric, all awaiting Bessie's attention. Bessie stood by the stove, her face lightly glistening with sweat as she pressed a heavy iron over a heap of freshly washed linens. Susan walked through the doorway, weary from her own day's work. She watched her daughter's focused movements, equal parts proud and worried.

"How much more you planning to do, honey?" Susan finally asked, arms crossed over her chest. "We still got beans and cabbage to tend to."

Bessie didn't pause her ironing, but a slight smile quirked at her mouth. "This work's here and now, Momma," she replied, echoing Susan's line. Her mom chuckled as Bessie's gaze remained on her task. "And so's daylight," Bessie added. "Those weeds'll wait—least 'til the kids get home from school."

Susan raised an eyebrow, stepping farther into the room. "You plan on using Charlie to gettin' that to town t'amorrow?" she asked.

"Sure enough," Bessie replied, switching to a fresh iron and wiping her brow. "Fixin' t o fill it back up if'n I can. If'n I get this done, the kids can ride to school in the mornin'."

Susan's eyes drifted to the last few clothes on the line, still damp and swaying gently in the breeze outside the window.

"You haven't heard back from Walter?" she asked softly, though she already knew the answer.

Bessie's hands pause briefly. "I told you, Momma—I'd let you know when I do."

Susan sighed and collapsed into a kitchen chair. She nodded toward the mason jar resting high on a shelf, where she knew Bessie was stashing her savings.

"Well, you've been working hard," she said. "How much you figure you got?"

Setting down the iron, Bessie reached for the jar, took it from the shelf, and peered inside. The stack of bills was modest but hard-earned, a physical measure of all her work.

"Got twenty-three dollars here, Momma," Bessie said, holding up the jar for her mother to see. "Same as yesterday. But after I get paid for all this, I'll have a li1 more than twenty-five."

She turned, stepped over to Susan, and wrapped her in a hug, feeling her mother's familiar warmth and strength.

"You're the one who taught me to work and save, Momma," she said, her voice thick with emotion. "Told me I ought to make something of myself. Not spend my life bowing and scraping."

Susan looked at her daughter, a soft smile playing on her lips. "You know we'll be all right," she said gently. "I'm proud of all my children, especially when they're doing well like you, John and Walter."

Bessie nodded, holding the mason jar in her hand, her eyes glinting with determination. "I'll leave some of this for you all when I head up to Chicago. Stay'n with John and Walter will make things easier."

A cotton field near Waxahachie, TX, circa 1913.

PART 2

Discovering Destiny

CHAPTER THREE

Chicago

———

Union Station in Chicago was the busiest place Bessie had ever been. The air carried the mingling scents of coal smoke from nearby locomotives, leather luggage, and the faint metallic tang of machinery. The building was a frenzy of movement, with travelers and porters hustling in every direction. She awkwardly pulled her suitcase through the crowd, looking around desperately for a familiar face. She stopped in frustration as her arms began to ache under the weight of her cargo.

"Help with the bags, ma'am?" a nearby familiar voice asked.

"Uh, no…," began Bessie awkwardly, eyes still focused on the crowd. Then suddenly, she turned to the speaker. "No, sir—Oh, Walter!"

He stood straight and tall, composed in his crisp Pullman Porter uniform. Bessie dropped her bags and rushed into his arms, engulfing him in a joyful, relieved hug. Walter laughed, squeezing her back tightly, glad to finally have her close.

They chatted happily on their way out of the station and through the streets of Chicago on the way to Walter's apartment. Walter smiled at Bessie's reactions to the tall buildings and rambling streetcars. Bronzeville's streets were lined with a mix of buildings—brick apartment complexes, modest single-family homes, and rows of narrow storefronts. The architecture reflected Chicago's working-class character with sturdy three-story flats, narrow alleys where children played, and laundry lines stretched between windows. Sidewalks were busy with residents, and the clamor of urban life filled the air. Bessie gasped at the sight of the elevated train.

"It's not Waxahachie, is it?" he joked.

They turned into the alcove of a brick apartment building and passed through a heavy wooden door into the hallway. Then Walter, with Bessie's bags in hand, led her up a narrow stairway lined with modest decor, the paint slightly chipped along the walls. Bessie followed, taking in everything around her in wonderment.

"Just a lil further—number 408," Walter said as he reached the door. He unlocked it and swung it open, motioning her inside. The apartment was a small, cozy space, kissed by the sunlight streams through windows with a view to the alley. Walter set Bessie's bags down and gestured to the front of the apartment.

"This front room's gonna be yours," he said, pointing to a small bedroom with a neatly made bed. "John and I'll share the back. Door at the end—that's the toilet 'n all. Big city living, huh? We got indoor plumbing!"

He chuckled as Bessie smiled, clearly impressed. She felt excited and relieved to be with Walter but couldn't help but feel like a fish out of water. After a good night's sleep, Bessie and Walter enjoyed breakfast at the small kitchen table with the newspaper spread open between them. Walter tapped the page with pride.

"I get the paper off the train most every day," he said, nodding at the headline. "This is The Defender. Best paper in the city."

Bessie looked up, eyebrows raised. "They got ads for jobs?"

Walter's expression turned serious. "They do, but most of

them here on the South Side are for domestic work. And I know you didn't come all this way to be washing shirts."

"I certainly did not," Bessie replied firmly.

Walter leaned forward, his voice a little softer. "Thing is Bessie, folks like us are taking the jobs white folks don't want. And they ain't too happy about it."

Bessie nodded, but her eyes showed a hint of defiance as she read the classifieds. "If'n they don't want to do them, what's wrong with us do'in 'em?"

"Well, we's doing them cheaper 'n they was an' takin' new jobs so they ain't any too happy."

Walter touched Bessie's hand to make sure she was listening. "Just want you to know. This ain't the south. You can be out at night 'n not get beat but there's still areas best not be going. You'll know'm when you see 'm. This area we're in here is called Bronzeville. Used to be called 'The Black Belt' or worse. Things are a whole lot better, but the race has a long way to go."

Bessie met his eyes with a quiet resilience. "Well, I don't gotta take the first thing that comes up, so I'm not scrubbing floors or shirts. Let me get my feet on the ground, and we'll see."

Bessie spent the next few days exploring the city and Walter's neighborhood. She stopped at a dress shop and admired the beautiful clothing on display, but the price tags made her wince. At the corner grocery store, she marveled at the shelves stocked with abundant fresh produce. At the fish market, she watched in astonishment as the workers tossed fish between them with practiced ease, calling out orders as they worked.

Passing a barber shop, she paused to peer inside through the window. She witnessed a manicurist finishing up the nails of a well-dressed customer who handed her a shiny dollar tip. Bessie's eyes linger on the scene, the wheels turning in her mind.

The next day, Bessie headed to the Burnham School of Beauty and Culture. The building was stunningly decorated with bright, colorful signs advertising classes in beauty and culture. With a steady breath, she stepped inside. Posters showing elegant hairstyles, manicured nails, and other sophisticated styles adorned the walls. Behind the counter, a young receptionist with impeccable grooming smiled as Bessie approached.

"Good day, ma'am. How can I help you?" the receptionist asked, her tone warm and welcoming.

"I'd like to enroll," Bessie replied, looking around at the signs with mixed excitement and nerves. "Could you tell me about the courses and tuition?"

The receptionist nodded and pulled out a few pamphlets. "The basic course lasts six weeks and costs eight dollars."

Bessie chuckled, shaking her head with a sigh. "That's a lotta shirts and sheets—but it looks like it'll be worth it."

The receptionist looked puzzled, not understanding the joke, but smiled politely and handed her the enrollment papers. Bessie reached into her coin purse, removed the folded bills, and handed them over to the receptionist. She felt ready to make her mark in this new city.

****

Bessie sat at a small table inside the glass window of the White Sox Barber Shop. Sunlight spilled over the manicure station of the lively establishment. Like most barbershops of the time, it was a vibrant community hub where gentlemen swapped baseball stories, debated sports strategies, and made friendly wagers on the next season. The Victrola provided a background of jazz tunes as a mix of devoted baseball fans, local workers, and the occasional White Sox team players waited in leather chairs for their turn to get a straight-razor shave, a traditional trim, or a daring new haircut. Typically, every seat was always occupied, and the hum of clippers and snips of scissors filled the space with a constant buzz as the faint smell of hair tonic and cologne wafted through the air. Outside, the sidewalk was busy with sharply dressed Black men and women, all in their Sunday best despite it being an ordinary weekday afternoon. Many people passing by slowed down when they saw Bessie in the window. Her polished appearance turned more than a few heads.

She didn't look like the woman who arrived in Chicago a year earlier. Her hair was now impeccably styled, her makeup subtle but alluring, and her sleek dress hinted at modern fashion without screaming for attention. It was enough to catch the eyes of the two men standing on the corner across the street, smoking cigars together. Their gazes shifted in unison to Bessie.

Robert Abbott, thirty-five, and every bit the newspaperman in his trim suit and relaxed but firm stance, nodded down at his hands with a sly grin. Despite his formal apparel, his face had a rugged look that was softened by the sienna color of his eyes. His companion, Jessie Binga, was slightly older and a sleek, handsome man. He leaned on a polished walking stick, raising an eyebrow at Robert's sudden interest in grooming.

"My nails are an absolute mess," Robert remarked, his tone almost conspiratorial. "I believe I'm overdue for a manicure."

Jessie tilted his head with an amused grin, catching sight of Bessie through the window. "Manicure? Robert, you've never had a manicure in your…" he trailed off, now understanding. "You know," he added, smirking as he lifted his cigar to his mouth, "I was going to say something about the condition of your hands, but I didn't want to embarrass you."

Robert chuckled. His face was warm with a hint of

sheepishness. Extinguishing his cigar and tucking it into a case, he crossed the street, heading straight for the barber shop's door with a newfound purpose. He pushed the door open, and the bell above gave a soft chime as he entered.

Through the window, Jessie watched as Robert hung his coat and hat on the nearby coat tree before striding up to the manicure station. Bessie rose gracefully to greet him, her smile measured, professional, but unmistakably welcoming.

Robert extended his hand in a greeting. "My oh my, what a delightful star of beauty," he said. "My name is Robert Abbott. And you are…?"

"Miss Bessie Coleman," Bessie replied, her voice steady as a slight hint of a blush crept onto her cheeks.

Robert's eyes sparkled with mischief. "I detect a foreign tone," he teased. "From what part of Spain have you recently arrived?"

Bessie tilted her head, amusement flickering in her gaze. "Newly arrived from the wilds of Texas, Mr. Abbott," she returned with a smirk. "But far enough from the border that I don't speak Spanish."

Robert smiled a little wider, appreciating her quick wit. "Well, Miss Coleman, I have a feeling you can do something about these horrible nails of mine," Robert teased.

She gestured for him to sit. He settled into the client's chair, extending his hand. She took it gently, examining the roughness of his skin. She lifted her eyebrows slightly at his fingers, which were free of calluses.

"My, such rough and damaged skin," she noted, her smile widening with playful curiosity. "Surely you're working the cutting floor at the stockyards."

Robert shook his head, charmed again by her apparent intelligence and humor. "No, no, my dear. Nothing so physically taxing," he replied. "I spend my days cutting to the truth and lifting up the race."

Bessie glanced up from his hand with a knowing smile. "I recognized you as you entered, sir."

"Please," Robert interjected, realizing he was correct about Bessie's cleverness. "Call me Robert."

She shook her head, a touch of teasing in her voice. "Since we just met, I think Mr. Abbott is more appropriate." Her eyes flicked toward the window. "And who is that gentleman I saw you with?"

Robert turned, glancing out toward the corner where Jessie still lingered, cigar in hand, occasionally looking over with casual curiosity. Bessie read the surprised expression on Robert's face.

"Oh, you think that window only goes one way?" she quipped, arching an eyebrow.

He gave a low laugh, enjoying her sharpness. "That, Miss Coleman, is the raconteur banker, Mr. Jessie Binga. I assure you; he'll be by in a few days."

Bessie's brow lifted with a glimmer of curiosity. "Raconteur, you say?"

Robert smirked. "Well, most would say. But he spends his days shifting papers and cutting checks."

She returned to his hand, carefully filing his nails, yet her eyes twinkled with intrigue. "That, and a snappy profile."

Robert leaned back in the chair, chuckling. "The 'Binga Bank' is his," he informed her, voice low and conspiratorial. "He's well sought after, so beware his smooth-talking ways. But, of course, you probably have another young beau to chase him off," he finished with a measured gaze.

Bessie didn't look up, realizing he was baiting her. Bessie's circle of friends had grown through the barber shop and Walter's introductions and she did indeed have a beau. Mason Adams was a fine young man and a trustworthy companion for a night out on the town.

Many evenings, Bessie and her friends piled into Mason's Model T Ford, and he maneuvered it along the busy Chicago streets, engine purring as they rolled up to the Dreamland Club. They joined the stream of well-dressed patrons heading inside, laughter and jazz spilling from the open door. Inside, the club was vibrant and electric with energy. A low light washed over the tables, casting everything in shades of amber and shadow as a lively band played on stage, filling the room with the infectious beat of the city's newest jazz. Bessie was captivated, her gaze dancing across the scene as Mason led the group to a table near the front. No sooner had they settled than a silver tray appeared, a bottle of champagne nestled in ice resting upon it, along with a small note. Across the room, a handsome admirer lifted his glass in a silent toast, eyes twinkling with admiration.

Mason's jaw tightened, but he forced a cordial smile, nodding back in acknowledgment. Bessie noticed and hid a grin, giving him a gentle nudge to playfully reassure him of her dedication. Mason softened, watching her as she raised her glass and clinked it lightly with her friends, who were all brimming with laughter and confidence.

Later, Bessie was at the bar and shared a brief, friendly exchange with a gentleman leaning in too eagerly. But as the clock crept toward closing, she broke off from the conversation, glancing over her shoulder to see Mason waiting, his steady gaze fixed on her. She waved him over with a bright smile, her friends rallying to follow her as they made their way to the door.

Outside, a new poster for the night's headliner in a neighboring club caught Bessie's attention. Cab Calloway was to appear next door. Bessie paused, glancing back at the club entrance, her eyes lighting up excitedly at the sight. Mason read her face immediately, gave her a kind smile, and motioned her inside the neighboring club with a teasing bow. Bessie's friends followed them jovially. It would be a late night for everyone!

As Cab Calloway took the stage and filled the club with his infectious rhythms, Bessie and Mason were soon swept onto the dance floor, moving in sync with the beat, feet tapping, bodies swaying. Bessie laughed, spinning under Mason's hand, her joy as bright and vibrant as the music filling the room. The hours drifted by, and the night blurred into a whirl of movement and melody. Finally, Mason led her into the calm, cool air of the early morning.

In front of Walter's apartment, he held the car door open as she stepped out onto the sidewalk, the last strains of the night's music still humming in her mind. Leaning forward, she planted a quick peck on his cheek, murmuring a warm thank you before disappearing into the apartment building.

The morning sun was merciless as it streamed through a small gap in Bessie's curtains, harsh and unforgiving as it woke her. The alarm clock rang out, its sharp, grating sound cutting through her haze of sleep. Blinking as she took in the sunlight, Bessie's head was filled with exciting memories from the night before. She hurried through her morning routine, softly humming a tune from the night before.

City of Chicago, circa 1920.

CHAPTER FOUR

Changes

———

She arrived at the barber shop just on time, her hair only slightly less pristine than usual. The barber shop buzzed with its usual mid-morning energy, the hum of conversation mingling with the snip of scissors and the scrape of razors. Bessie's first customer entered, and she focused on the businessman's hand, working the file methodically as she chatted with him, the rhythm of her work steady and precise. Around her, the shop was alive as the city, a place of routine and steady trade.

Suddenly, the door burst open, clanging against the bell as it swung wide. Every head turned as a man rushed in, waving a copy of the *Chicago Defender*. It was Kyle, a familiar businessman in his thirties and one of the shop's regulars. He cut a well-dressed figure in his dark suit but was disheveled and breathless today.

"Jimmy! Jimmy! Where are you, man?" Kyle shouted, his voice filling the shop, lifting heads from chairs and causing hands to pause mid-shave. Even Bessie stopped. Her gaze followed the line of curious looks toward the source of the commotion.

From the back office, James Bridgeman, the shop's manager, poked his head out. He was a solidly built man with a belly that spoke to years of hearty meals. His age was betrayed by his graying hair and lines etched deep into his dark skin. His eyebrows knitted together in irritation as he emerged fully, hands planted on his hips.

"Kyle, what's gotcha all excited?" he asked, his voice carrying a heavy, fatherly tone as if already preparing to bring calm to whatever storm Kyle was trying to stir up.

"It's war! War, Jimmy!" Kyle cried, his arm outstretched, holding up the newspaper triumphantly.

James gave him a skeptical look. "Of course, there's a war, Kyle. They been killin' each other over in Europe for a couple years now."

Kyle's face lit with excitement, and he ignored James's skepticism. "But we's in it now! President Wilson's declared war on Germany!" He waved the paper again, and heads turned with renewed interest. Murmurs swept through the room as patrons exchanged glances, the reality of his words sinking in.

James frowned, his expression shifting from irritation to contemplation. "Has he now?" he mused, his tone quiet as if weighing each word. "I 'spect that's gonna change things 'round here in short order."

Kyle nodded, leaning in as though he were speaking to each person in the shop individually. "They callin' up the Eighth," he said, a flicker of pride in his voice. "Callin' for volunteers, too."

James's eyes narrowed, and he scanned the shop, his gaze zeroing in on the younger barbers, most of whom were watching Kyle with a spark of excitement. "Don't any of you get no ideas," he warned, his voice sharp. "I got enough trouble as it is—don't need any of you gettin' patriotic on us now."

A few of the younger barbers who had straightened up now returned to their former posture with dimmed enthusiasm under James's steady glare. Others exchanged glances, their eyes still glinting with a faint light of possibility. James seemed to regain his calm, and though his voice softened, his gaze turned hard.

"'Sides, what's this country been doin' for you all lately?" he asked, the question hanging in the air, laced with frustration and resignation that went unspoken but understood by every man there. His words stirred a mix of tension and truth, the unspoken question resonating with the weight of their shared experience.

Kyle stood undeterred, his eyes burning with conviction. "At least the Eighth got officers of the race. Only colored unit that's got that," he said firmly, pride swelling in his voice. "Don't need no white man tell a black man how to fight."

The room grew still as Kyle's words sank in, the usual hum of the shop muted by a new sense of purpose and pride. And in the silence, a resolve began to take shape, subtle and quiet, a new determination simmering in the air as the weight of choice and consequence echoed silently through every corner of the barbershop.

✳✳✳

Bessie pushed open the door to her apartment, stepping aside to let Susan, Georgia, Isaiah, Elois, Walter, and John file in. Everyone was laden with bags that had seen better days—battered suitcases and worn duffels, the marks of their long journey. Georgia clutched a small, rattling cage, which she set down carefully on the floor before unlatching the door. Katos slipped out, whiskers twitching as he took in the unfamiliar space before darting under the couch for shelter.

Susan plopped down on the nearby couch and ran her hand across its arm, her fingers sinking into its soft fabric. She sighed in admiration as though this moment of comfort was something she hadn't dared hope for on the bumpy, dust-filled roads they'd left behind.

"Whoo, what a journey," Susan said, catching her breath. "All that country just whizzing by." A slow smile crept onto her face. "Would've taken us a month or more with ole Charlie draggin' us up here."

She looked around the apartment as if surveying a palace. "My goodness, my children done well," Susan said, beaming with pride.

After several months of begging, Susan had finally accepted her children's invitation to join them in the big city. Between more work opportunities, better schools, and uniting the family, making the move seemed like the right thing to do. Now, Walter and John hovered near her, hands stuffed in their pockets, glancing at each other. They stood close to their mother, unable to hide the pride and anxious energy crackling between them as something important weighed on their minds. Susan leaned back, oblivious, looking around the room with satisfaction.

"Back together as a family," she murmured, her voice soft with wonder. "Lord have mercy, never thought I'd see the day."

Bessie glanced at her brothers, feeling the tension of what they all needed to say. Nobody wanted to be the first to say it. She forced a small smile, her voice gentle.

"Yeah, Momma, this is great."

She shot Walter an imploring look. *Tell her now,* it seemed to say. Walter cleared his throat, and John straightened beside him, hands dropping from his pockets.

"Momma, you know how those folks over in France have been at war with Germany for a while now, right?" John began carefully. "You've heard about that?"

Susan nodded slowly. "Reverend mentioned something

'bout that. Said it weren't our nevermind 'cause it's over cross the ocean."

Walter took a deep breath. "Well, Momma, that's changed. President Wilson's got America in the war now. He declared war on Germany."

Susan blinked, the news registering slowly, her brows knitting together in confusion. "So what's that to us?" she asked, shaking her head. "Ain't nobody here in the army."

Walter and John exchanged glances before John looked at his mother directly, the truth heavy on his tongue.

"Yeah...well, Momma, me and Walter joined up. We're in the Eighth, come next week."

Susan's face fell. "Oh no. No, no, no. I didn't raise my boys to be soldiers," she said, her voice dropping to a choked whisper. She sat up, her hands gripping the edge of the couch as though she could hold onto them that way. "Gonna go off 'cross the world fer what? Gonna die for some king or queen ain't yours."

Walter lowered himself to her level, resting a hand on her arm. "I wouldn't worry about that, Momma," he said, his voice soothing if unconvincing. "They're gonna use us to load boxes and supplies. Ain't no white man trust a colored boy to fight for 'em."

But Susan's face was still full of distress, a flicker of relief visible on Bessie's face though the worry remained beneath the surface. John's voice broke through the silence, determined yet trying to reassure her. "It pays thirty dollars a month each. We're sending most of it home, straight to you."

Susan's lip trembled. "Didn't raise my boys to go kill nobody," she whispered, holding back a tear. "I don't need no money that bad."

Walter squatted down beside her, meeting her eyes. "We're gonna be fine, Momma," he said firmly. "We'll write as often as we can, and Bessie here, she'll read 'em to you."

Susan's face softened. Her shoulders fell with a resigned acceptance, understanding that the decision had already been made.

"Maybe," she said quietly, "or maybe I'm gonna learn to read. It's about time, I reckon." She looked around at the others, gathering strength in their presence. "Georgia, Isaiah, Elois, Bessie, you all gonna teach me. I'll even write to you," she added, forcing a small, hopeful smile at John and Walter. "Just you wait and see."

Walter leaned in and wrapped his arms around her. Susan held onto him tightly, her face wet, pressing a hand against his back. "You promise me you're gonna look after each other," she whispered.

John nodded. "That's a promise, Momma."

****

Robert Abbott was becoming one of Bessie's favorite customers. Her hands deftly worked over his nails as they exchanged familiar conversation. She glanced at the newspaper folded on the corner of the table, her mind tracing back to her brothers' departure.

"I see by your paper the boys are doing well," she said apprehensively. "Is that what's really happening?"

Robert's gaze met hers steadily. "I assure you our reports are as accurate as any other," he said, his voice carrying the quiet authority of his position. "The Eighth got folded into the three-oh-seventh. The army was so confident in their abilities, they seconded them to the French."

Bessie's brow furrowed slightly. "I take it that means the white generals just wanted to get rid of our boys 'cause they don't trust them."

Robert smiled, his gaze still calm, like a man used to seeing things from all angles. "That might be one way of looking at it. But they've acquitted themselves quite well."

He nodded toward the paper, the headline angled so she could see it. "Schwarze Teufel is the name the Germans have given them. Black devils. So far, the units have been outstanding."

Bessie's eyes flicked to another section of the paper, a photograph of a man with an intense, sharp gaze. His name, Eugene Bullard, stood out in bold under the headline.

"Looks like airplanes are more and more important," she said. "Lots of articles 'bout them these days."

"Developing, romantic instruments of war," Robert replied, his tone laced with irony. "Good copy. Sells papers."

Bessie smiled slightly. The edge of skepticism was not lost on her. She glanced again at Bullard's photo.

"This Bullard fella looks quite dashing."

"From Columbus, Georgia," Robert said as though supplying details of an old friend. "Fighting for the French a while now. Used to be a boxer. Pretty good one, too. Headstrong."

Bessie paused, her hands momentarily still, and lifted her eyes to meet his. "How come he's the only one of the race who's become a pilot? Even white ladies have been flying. How come no men or ladies of the race have become pilots?"

Robert smiled thoughtfully, his eyes crinkling at the corners. "We're hoping for that someday."

Bessie's gaze held steady. "How much good is hoping?" she asked, her voice low, almost daring. "Flying is the future. We just gonna let it pass us by?"

Robert tilted his head, the weight of his words settling with calm certainty. "It all starts with the idea," he said. "With the idea comes the dream, usually followed by a lot of work. Everything, step by step."

Bessie looked down at his hands again, the world of endless possibility lingering around them in a neither empty nor idle silence.

CHAPTER FIVE

Signs of the Times

———

Lake Michigan gleamed in the hot July sun, waves lapping gently against the sand as white Chicagoans lounged along the beach, savoring the carefree joys of summer. Laughter, shouts, and occasional splashes filled the air, blending with the sounds of picnics and children playing. The shoreline, an idyllic leisure scene, stretched as far as the eye could see, its crowded edges humming with life.

But as a small group of black youths strolled along the edge of the sand, the relaxed air shifted, replaced by tension as white beachgoers eyed them with suspicion. Heads turned, glances exchanged, and murmurs of discomfort rippled through the crowd. Eyes narrowed, and soon, people rose from their blankets and chairs, clustering into an impenetrable wall that loomed in the youths' path.

A montage of moments unfolded suddenly, each scene escalating with alarming speed. White men gathered, blocking the black teens' route. Words were exchanged, voices were raised, gestures pointed sharply, and each party entrenched itself in indignation. A white man pushed his way to the front, a baseball bat clutched in his hand—a makeshift weapon borrowed from a nearby child. One of the black girls in the group tugged at her friends, urging them to turn back, her voice thick with worry. But the taunts continued, with barbs thrown from both sides until the tension boiled over.

QUEEN OF THE SKIES

Shoving turned to fists. A rock flew from somewhere in the chaos, striking a white man in the head, and he stumbled, blood trickling down his temple. The bat swung wildly in retaliation, landing heavily against a black youth's chest, the impact knocking him to the sand. A garbage can hurled through the air, landing with a heavy thud amidst the fray.

Then the police arrived, wading into the melee with raised billy clubs. But their blows fell only on the black teens, who scattered, some dragging injured friends as they fled, one youth slumped unconscious between them.

When the dust settled, white beachgoers relaxed, tending to their scrapes and bruises as though nothing had happened. Ice packs and makeshift bandages adorned their heads and arms as they tried to reclaim the day's peace. Officer O'Brian, a gruff, middle-aged cop with a hard-edged smirk, ambled over to one of the beachgoers, nursing a dark bruise on his forehead.

"That was a hell of a row, weren't it?" O'Brian drawled, nodding at the man's injury. "You got yourself a real nice shiner there."

The man, a burly thirty-something with a black eye already darkening, chuckled ruefully. "Sure as hell," he muttered. "They thought they'd bring their black asses down here. Guess they got other ideas now."

"Yeah," said Office O'Brian amicably. "Gonna think twice before they try that again. T'aint any signs, but they know what's what. If they didn't know, they sure as hell know now."

The injured man nodded as best he could without jarring himself. "They got their own beach south of twenty-fifth street. They can damn well stay there."

Across the beach, a tiny raft drifted closer to shore. Its young occupants were three black boys, all barely into their teens. They were oblivious to the simmering hostility that awaited them on the sand. Officer O'Brian caught sight of the raft, and a glint of irritation darkened his gaze.

"Oh, what the hell is this now?" he sneered. "They got themselves a damn navy?

Nearby, a younger beachgoer, barely eighteen, shouted toward the raft, his tone thick with contempt. "Get outta here! Ain't ya seen what we just did to them others?"

On the raft, Eugene Williams—a wiry eleven-year-old, shirtless under the blazing sun—squinted toward shore.

"Calvin," he called to his raft mate, his voice rising with curiosity and a hint of concern, "What they sayin'? Why they all bunched up like that?"

Calvin, slightly older, shook his head, his bare shoulders stiffening. "They seem mighty pissed 'bout somethin'," he replied, his eyes narrowing.

Donald, the third boy, looked back over his shoulder nervously. "Let's get the hell outta here," he muttered, and all three boys began paddling with their hands, splashing as they tried to steer the raft away from the hostile shore.

But back on land, Ben Townsman, a heavyset man clutching a beer bottle, grinned at the sight of the boys' panic. He took a swig, then let the bottle fly, laughing as it sailed through the air, narrowly missing the raft.

"Hell, let's make this fun!" he shouted, spurring on the crowd. The eighteen-year-old snatched up a rock and hurled it, quickly joined by others, their stones arcing over the water in a hail of projectiles.

The boys ducked as best they could, but in the confusion, a stone struck Eugene square on the head. He gasped, clutching his head in pain, and then, with a sudden twist, he toppled forward, splashing into the lake. Donald's eyes widened in horror, reaching out instinctively toward his friend.

"Gene! Eugene!!" Donald cried, scanning the water as Calvin jumped in to find him, bobbing under the murky water in vain. But Eugene was gone, the lake's calm surface revealing nothing.

The crowd onshore reacted with mixed emotions, including cheers and horrified screams. Many were silent. Others turned to leave, guilt mingling with shock. Officer O'Brian, frozen next to Townsman, finally spoke, his voice low with anger.

"You might want to make yourself real scarce for a while," he muttered darkly. "Startin' with right the hell now."

Townsman stammered, still dazed. "I...I didn't mean to—"

"But ya did." O'Brian's gaze was cold. "Now get the hell outta here. Move your ass!"

Later, a Chicago Tribune delivery van rattled through the city's streets, sending bundles of newspapers thudding onto the sidewalks. A bold and grim single headline screamed from the front page: *RACE RIOTS SPREAD ACROSS COUNTRY, HEAVY LOSS OF LIFE.*

That evening, as the city simmered with unrest, a streetcar rattled to a halt in front of a mob of white men brandishing clubs and torches. The car's passengers—black Chicagoans returning from work or visiting family—looked out in alarm as the men surrounded the vehicle, faces twisted in anger, fists gripping makeshift weapons.

Inside, Bessie and Susan sat side by side on a wooden bench. Susan was smiling softly, distracted by a small child across from her who babbled happily, oblivious to the rising tension. Then, with a shattering crack, a rock smashed through the window behind Bessie, sending shards of glass scattering across the seat and barely missing the child. Bessie jolted, instinctively shielding Susan as passengers ducked and murmured in fear.

She shot to her feet, clutching Susan's arm. "We gotta be going, Momma!" she urged, her voice thick with urgency.

Susan looked up and spotted the mob pressing in around the streetcar. She stood, a fierce look flashing across her face, but her legs were shaky, and Bessie tugged her toward the rear door.

"Go, child," Susan insisted, her voice steely even in fear. "You wait'n on me you back'n up."

Bessie grabbed Susan's arm and compelled her forward. Together, the two women slipped out the back of the car, ducking through the growing chaos and running down the street as the city around them teetered on the brink of violence. They hid in the shadows when they heard a mob swelling around the corner, pressing themselves against a rickety fence near a narrow alleyway. Bessie's face was pale with confusion, her mind reeling as she tried to understand the sudden, brutal turn of events.

"Momma, what do you think that's all about?" she whispered, her voice tense.

Susan's gaze was steely, and her expression was one of hardened experience. "Don't know," she replied grimly, "but anytime you see white folks with bats 'n torches, it's time to be somewhere else."

Bessie and Momma had escaped just moments before a flaming torch burst through one of the shattered windows of the streetcar, landing with a shower of sparks in the center aisle. The flames caught on the worn seats, licking at the walls, spreading quickly through the narrow confines. Passengers scrambled to escape, leaping from the windows as the streetcar transformed into an inferno, its orange glow lighting the darkening streets. Other mobs chased lone black men on the streets while brandishing weapons. In another part of the city, a white man driving a Model T was stopped by four black men pointing a shotgun at him. The white man raised his revolver, but in an instant, a shotgun blast shattered the windshield. The driver slumped over, blood dripping down his face. Meanwhile, a Baptist church mysteriously erupted in flames, and black men and women formed a desperate bucket brigade as they fought to save it from destruction.

The front page of The Defender landed on doorsteps across the city, a bold headline shouting the tragic news: *RACE RIOT IN CITY. COLORED YOUTH DROWNED AT BEACH.* A day later, the front page cried out again amid the growing chaos: GOVERNOR DECLARES EMERGENCY, MILITIA DEPLOYED.

White militia troops arrived, their uniforms stained with sweat and their bayonets glinting in the dim light as they pressed back the mobs. Several days and lots of deaths and injuries later, *The Defender* proclaimed: *RIOTS OVER! 38 KILLED, 500 INJURED! RED SUMMER ENDING!*

As Bessie helped her mother read the headline aloud, Susan sighed.

"It was like this in Texas. Now here."

Bessie echoed her mother's sigh. There had to be someplace far away from the violence and hatred between blacks and whites. Someplace where she could feel peace and freedom. She remembered standing in Johanson's cotton field so many years ago. The hawk. The sky. The photo of Bullard, a black pilot. The sky was peace. The sky was free. Now all she had to do was get there.

PART 3

Wings of Change

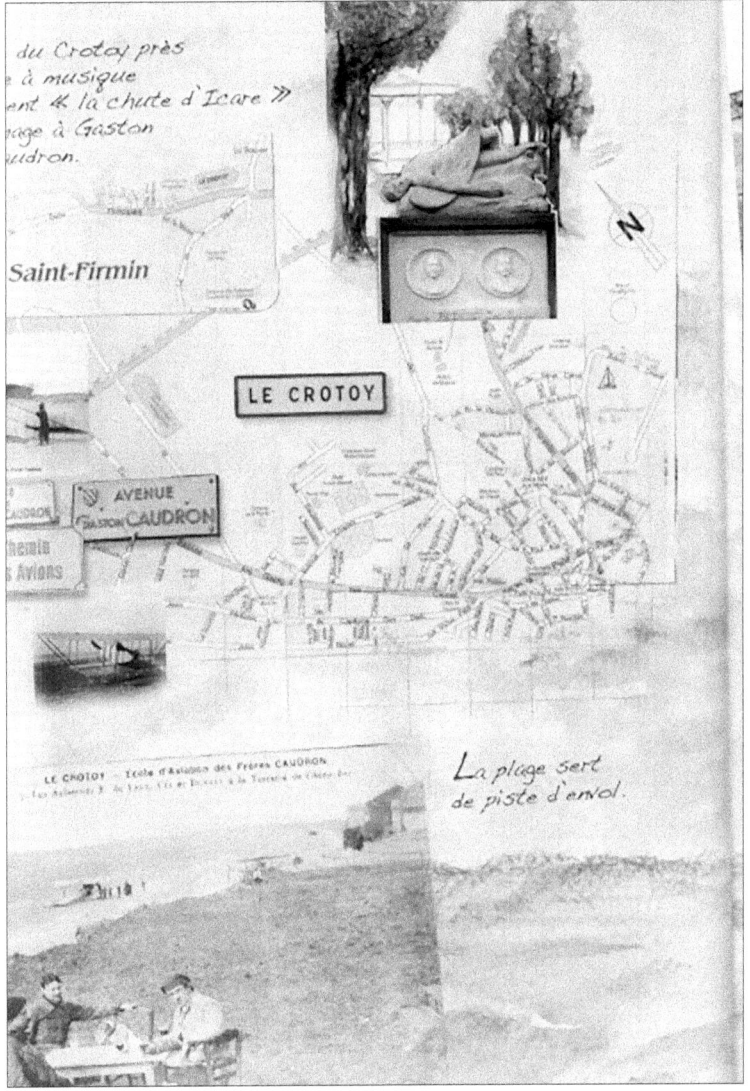

CHAPTER SIX

Choices and Chances

B essie sat at the kitchen table with a letter held loosely in her hand. Her expression was one of weary resignation as she put the letter down atop a small pile just as Susan entered the room, her arms full of envelopes.

"Mail's here. Three of 'em," Susan announced, her tone forcedly upbeat.

Bessie gave a humorless smile. "I can only guess. More rejections," she muttered, barely glancing at the letters before dropping her gaze to the pile on the table.

Susan watched her daughter, concern furrowing her brow. "Honey, how long you been after this?"

Bessie sighed. "A little over a month," she replied, her voice barely above a whisper.

Susan's tone turned sharper. "Does anyone else know what you been after? You ain't told no one else?"

Bessie shook her head. "No, Momma. Walter and John would be all over me if they did."

Susan looked at her, eyes narrowing. "Why'd you figure on doing this, anyway?"

Bessie's gaze drifted to the window with a distant expression. "I don't know," she murmured. "A conversation with a friend got me going. Got me dreaming..."

Her voice trailed off as she glanced back down at the three letters Susan had placed on the table. Susan eyed her, the soft lines of her face creased with motherly worry. "You don't know anything 'til you open them."

With a sigh, Bessie picked up the envelopes, tearing each open in turn. Her expression grew darker with each rejection, letting two letters flutter to the floor.

"Like I said," she muttered bitterly, "No again and again. No women. No coloreds."

Susan's face softened, but her voice held a quiet strength. "You ain't quittin,' are you?"

Bessie slumped in her chair, looking down at her empty hands, then at the last unopened letter. "Don't know, Momma. Running outta schools and ideas."

Susan gave her a long look, her face unreadable. Then, her lips curled into a slight smile. "See which one fills up first."

Susan pointed to the last unopened letter. Bessie sighed, opened the envelope, and met Susan's eyes. A silent exchange of understanding passed between them. Susan pulled her daughter into a hug, their silent embrace heavy with unspoken determination.

Bessie took a deep, steadying breath, then clenched her fists, her hand slamming against the table with a newfound resolve. "No," she declared, her voice steady and fierce. "Not as long as I've got a breath. I'm not quitting. If there's a will, there's gotta be a way."

A tear slipped down Susan's cheek as she looked at her daughter with pride, her voice barely a whisper. "Where there's life, there's hope," she said softly.

Bessie nodded, determination shining in her eyes. "By God, I'm going to find a way."

****

Inside the barber shop, the buzz of clippers and the chatter of customers filled the air. Bessie sat at her work desk, carefully tending to a client's nails, her fingers nimble and precise. Across from her, Walter reclined in a cushioned chair, his hands resting idly. John sat nearby, next to Walter, awaiting his turn for a haircut and savoring the easy rhythm of the shop. Outside the glass windows, autumn leaves tumbled along the street, and people hurried by, bundled against the brisk October air. With a rare lull in her clients, Bessie was busying herself straightening her station.

Walter's eyes twinkled as he broke the silence. "So, Bessie, you're pretty good at making hands pretty. How come you never done mine?"

Bessie laughed, her gaze flicking to his hands. "Walter, you know I'm no quitter, but some hills are too steep to climb. Fixing those paws of yours would take a week!" she teased as Walter let out a chuckle, amused. "What am I gonna do for money in the meantime?"

Walter returned to his reading, but their conversation got John's attention. John joined in, leaning forward with a sly grin. "Leave her alone, Walter. She's gotta sit here looking pretty in this window 'til some handsome boy comes and sweeps her off her feet."

"I'm hardworking. Nothing wrong with that," replied Bessie, refusing to take her brother's bait.

"Oh, you're a hard worker," John replied thoughtfully, "but you could be working hard at something better."

Bessie stopped lining up the nail lacquer and glanced over, intrigued. "Like what?" she asked calmly.

John sighed, his tone taking on a wistful note. "Well, like the women in France. Over there, they've got careers. They're businesswomen—they run things." He paused, sensing he was striking a nerve. With a cocky grin, he added, "Even a couple of 'em learned to fly airplanes. Ain't no colored girl ever gonna do that."

Bessie listened for a minute, staring off into the distance. Then, silently, she rose from her seat and headed for the coat rack with steely determination. She grabbed her light coat from the hook near the door and threw it over her shoulders with determination. Her brothers stared after her in amusement, and some of the barbers and their customers were now watching her, too.

"Bessie?" Walter said, watching her carefully. "Where you going?"

Jimmy stopped snipping and looked up from his customer. "Yeah, I'd like to hear this too," he said tentatively.

Bessie's hand was on the doorknob now, but she turned around to answer her brother.

"I'm going to start working hard at something else," she replied, looking at John. "Now." Then she looked up at Jimmy, whose mouth was wide open in amazement. "Sorry, Jimmy. I gotta go."

And with that, she walked out the door and into what she thought might soon be a new life.

CHAPTER SEVEN

New Directions

———

Bessie was lost in thought as she walked down the sidewalk. Without even thinking, she found herself heading for the bustling newsroom of *The Defender*. She entered boldly, her coat swishing as she passed rows of reporters hunched over their desks, typing furiously or scribbling notes. Several male reporters glanced her way, nodding admiringly at her determined expression. The steady clatter of the teletype machines filled the room as she reached an open doorway marked "Office of Editor."

She tapped on the doorframe, and Robert Abbott, deep in thought at his desk, looked up. Seeing her, he smiled warmly.

"I hope I'm not disturbing you, sir," Bessie said, her voice steady but respectful.

Abbott's eyes sparkled. "That would take some doing, young lady. Come in. Have a seat."

Bessie entered, her heart pounding as she took the seat opposite him. She glanced around the office, catching sight of a calendar on the wall with the date marked October 12.

"They said you had an open-door policy. I guess they weren't kidding."

"If you want to know what's going on, you have to talk to people. The fewer barriers, the better," Robert replied cordially. "So, to what do I owe the pleasure?"

Bessie leaned forward. "I've been thinking about our conversation about aviation."

Abbott's eyebrows raised with interest. "And?"

"I want to learn to fly. And I want to start a flying school. A school for the race—not just for the race, but open to anyone." Bessie replied, her words gathering momentum.

Robert's attention sharpened as he took in her proposal, nodding thoughtfully. "And how does this come about? "Have you applied to any schools?"

Bessie swallowed, glancing down as her excitement dimmed slightly. "I've applied to every school I could find," she admitted. "They won't teach women—they say we're too panicky or lack concentration." Her voice grew quieter. "And because I'm black. They were polite but implied that people of the race aren't… smart enough."

Abbott leaned back in his chair, a look of quiet determination settling over his face. After a moment, he murmured, "France."

Bessie blinked, confused. "Excuse me, sir?"

Robert leaned forward again, his gaze steady. "You, my dear, aren't going to find a single school or white soul here in America to teach you. Absurd, seeing how we invented the airplane, but that's the truth of it." He paused, letting the words sink in. "But France—they are the center of aviation today. Equal or better in most things technical and certainly regarding matters of the race."

Bessie sat back, feeling the enormity of the idea. "France is pretty far away," she whispered.

Robert gave her a small smile. "It's closer than you think. But one step at a time. You'll need two things beyond your gumption."

Bessie's face brightened with hope but remained cautious.

"Only two things?"

"A considerable amount of money and fluency in French." Robert scribbled an address on a slip of paper and handed it to her. "As good as you are at your craft, you'll need a better-paying job to save up."

Bessie took the paper, glancing at the address. Robert continued, "I was just speaking with Jessie Binga. He's financing a new chili parlor on State Street, and they'll need a manager. Jessie... hcreby recommends you."

Bessie's smile widened as she realized the possibilities unfolding before her.

"As for *de parler de français,*" Robert added with a wink, "I'd suggest inquiring at the Berlitz School over on Wabash Avenue. The ads we've published show they're quite popular."

Bessie sat there, momentarily overwhelmed. "I... I have to say, this is an overwhelming gift."

Robert shook his head. "It's no gift. There's a lot of work ahead of you. You're going to earn every bit of it. Do the work, and the rest will follow."

****

Within days, Bessie's life had changed. She began work at the new Chili'n Parlor on State Street, making considerably more than her manicurist job. Bessie worked the cash register, handing change to customers with a bright smile. The place buzzed with patrons at the lunch counter and tables, enjoying hearty meals and the lively atmosphere. In the kitchen, cooks plated dishes and rang a bell for orders while servers moved swiftly between tables, balancing plates and calling orders to the back. Bessie was the manager and in charge of several

QUEEN OF THE SKIES

employees. Just like back home when she watched her younger siblings, nothing got past Bessie. When a young busboy, Sammy, stood at the counter's far end, sneaking a quick cigarette with a dishtub at his feet, Bessie's eyes narrowed as she saw him.

"Sammy!" she called sharply. "Dump that butt and get your butt out there! Tables don't clear themselves."

"Yes, Miss Coleman, I'm movin'," he muttered, stubbing out the cigarette and hurrying off.

Another customer approached, handing her his bill and some cash. She beamed at him. "Everything all right today?"

"Best on the whole South Side," he replied with a grin.

"Well, you come back and see us again real soon," Bessie said, her smile broadening as he nodded and walked out.

Later that night, in a small classroom at the Berlitz School, Bessie sat with a group of black students, all eager to learn. M. Meunier, a tall, dignified man with silver hair, stood at the chalkboard, guiding them through the basics of French. He wrote a phrase on the board and turned to the class.

"Say the English phrase in French, please. *The sun is shining brightly today.*

"*Le soleil brille de mille feux aujourd'hui,*" Bessie joined in with the other students.

"Very good," Meunier encouraged. "Now. It is very cold."

"*Il fait très froid,*" the students replied, their confidence growing with each repetition.

The instructor nodded approvingly. "Now, Bessie Coleman," he said, turning to her. "Despite the presence of the sun, it is very cold."

"*Malgré la présence du soleil, il fait très froid,*" Bessie replied perfectly. The instructor smiled at her. Although it was very different from English, Bessie picked up French very quickly and was getting excited about moving to a different country.

Meanwhile, Jessie Binga's bank office was silent after hours as Robert Abbott paced, enjoying a cigar with his friend. His long, unhurried, yet purposeful strides trailed back and forth across Jessie's floor. Jessie sat across his desk, his sharp gaze resting on Robert, a subtle curiosity etched in his eyes.

"So, you think she's worth the investment?" Jessie's voice was low but unwavering, each word measured.

Robert stopped and met his friend's gaze, a wry smile creeping into the corner of his mouth. "Absolutely. She's motivated as all hell. You know how hard she's working. You realize what it means for us if she succeeds?"

Jessie blew aromatic smoke into the air, absorbing Robert's enthusiasm. "I suppose, win or lose, you'll sell a bunch more papers." His tone was pragmatic, but there was a faint glint of humor there.

"It's more than just printing papers," Robert replied thoughtfully, leaning towards Jessie over the desk. "Here's someone who can make a difference to colored people everywhere. What she puts her mind to, she achieves." He gave Robert an even gaze across the desk. "We could be part of history in the making here," he said quietly.

Jessie smiled and nodded, accepting the point with effortless grace. "Okay. So how's her French?" he asked, leaning back languidly.

Robert switched smoothly to French, his words curling off his tongue with practiced ease. *"Aussi bon que le mien mais elle l'a appris en huit mois,"* he said before answering Jessie's blank stare with an English translation. "I'd say as good as mine, but it took me a few years, and she learned it in only eight months."

Jessie couldn't help but laugh, shaking his head. "You got me there, Robert. You know I don't parlay a single word of it," he said, chuckling.

"There's a school outside of Paris that'll take her," Robert continued, his voice calming as he leaned against the window ledge. "One foot in front of the other—that's how we get to where we're going."

Jessie rocked his chair back, eyes narrowing thoughtfully. "Guess we're gonna show 'em once and for all. We ain't gonna keep 'em down on the farm once we've seen Paree."

Robert met his friend's gaze, a quiet resolve threading through his voice. "Forward, Jessie, always forward. Ain't no going back."

Robert Abbott, American lawyer, newspaper publisher and editor, and founder of The Chicago Defender

Jessie Binga, prominent African American businessman and banker

CHAPTER EIGHT

Bessie Abroad

———

The light in Bessie's apartment cast a soft glow as Susan sat surrounded by her children, each face reflecting anticipation and encouragement. John, her eldest, leaned close, his gaze tender as he urged her on, his presence like an anchor.

She held an envelope addressed in a careful hand, her fingers brushing lightly over her name. Hesitantly, she opened it, drawing out the letter with deliberate care. She met John's eyes, offering it to him, but he shook his head gently, the edges of his lips lifting into a reassuring smile.

"You read it, Momma," he encouraged quietly.

"All right, I will," Susan said with determination. She took a breath to brace herself and then began. "Dear Momma, I got to New York with all my luggage in fine shape."

John's smile broadened, his quiet pride radiating like a warmth in the small room. Susan looked up, pausing to imagine Bessie on a bustling dock, surrounded by the organized chaos of porters shouting orders and taxis spilling out passengers. She could see her clutching her bags with purpose and a porter, with his face shaded beneath his cap, stepping forward to help her, gesturing toward the gangplank.

"The ship is so big," Susan read, continuing the letter. "It's longer than two city blocks. It's called the SS Im...." Susan trailed off, stumped by the big word.

"Imperator," finished John, encouragingly, over her shoulder.

"Everyone is very nice," Susan continued, "and I hope France is like this because nobody seems to care I'm of the race."

Again, she paused to see Bessie in her mind's eye, dressed for dinner with other passengers in evening wear like the pictures she had seen in Walter's newspapers. She imagined an integrated dining room with blacks and whites eating together. She continued with the letter.

"Momma, I don't know how I got so far from Texas. This world is so big; I hope I don't get lost in it."

Susan opened her mouth slightly, wanting to encourage her daughter aloud. Instead, she read on.

"The name of the school is *Le Ecole De Aviation Civil.* I think it's beautiful. So are the planes. It smells like machine oil and fresh grass here, and it seems like the sky is a beautiful blue for flying every day. When I first arrived, I saw two amazing planes. They were a Caudron G3 and a Breguet 14 biplane. It was so exciting to think I was going to learn to fly. Maybe someday I'll fly one. Momma, I miss you all and will write as much as I can. Kiss everyone for me. Love, your Bessie"

A calm fell over the room, and everyone shifted their position, relaxed now from having been on the edge of their seat with the letter. Susan closed her eyes and said a silent prayer for her daughter's safety so far away.

****

Antoine Dennis, director of the *Le Ecole De Aviation Civil,* appeared in the doorway, dressed in worn but sturdy flying garb. Bessie was seated in his office, and he approached her with a relaxed stride, nodding in greeting.

"Ah, Miss Coleman. We've been anticipating your arrival."

Bessie extended her hand, her smile warm yet reserved. "Mr. Dennis, a pleasure. Such a beautiful school. I can't wait to get started."

"Ah, yes, well. I'm afraid I have some less-than-pleasant news." His voice softened, a hint of sympathy in his tone.

Bessie's smile faltered, and her eyes searched his face. "Events?"

"Yes," Antoine began slowly. "Unfortunately, we've suffered some accidents in the last two weeks. Two students have come to grief."

Bessie's throat tightened. "I see, and...?"

Antoine sighed. "We can no longer accept students for flight lessons. However, I understand you've come a great distance, and I've made some arrangements for you. There's a competitor up north—a friend, actually. He runs Le Ecole d'Aviation des Freres Caudron, and he'll gladly accept your application."

Bessie forced her disappointment away and steadied her resolve. "Well, that being the case, I should head for... where is the school?"

"Le Crotoy," Antoine replied with an encouraging nod. "It's a beautiful little town. I'll arrange transport for you."

Le Crotoy was indeed a beautiful, quaint fishing village and budding seaside resort on the English Channel along the northern coast of France. Located on the Bay of the Somme, Le Crotoy was known for its unique southern exposure. It was a rarity along the French northern coastline, giving the area a charm and warmth that attracted artists, writers, and holidaymakers, much like the impressionist painters who captured its beauty in fleeting, vibrant strokes.

As Bessie walked down the worn path leading to the main

building at Le Ecole d'Aviation des Freres Caudron, the wind carried a faint tang of salt up from the beach below, drifting through the trees. She drank in the vastness of the sky and the hum of distant engines. The rhythmic crunch of sand beneath her boots felt grounding as she approached. Overhead, a Caudron G3 trainer cut through the sky, casting a fleeting shadow across her path. It was a sleek, lightweight biplane with stubby wings. Instinctively, Bessie's hands mimicked the plane's movements, her fingers tracing invisible lines, her gaze firmly locked onto the aircraft until it disappeared over the hill.

Nearby, René Caudron stood under a shade tree with a slight smile on his lips. He watched Bessie as she approached. His frame was slim, yet he had the kind of posture that spoke to years of discipline, his hands casually tucked into his pockets as he observed the newcomer with curious intent.

"Miss Coleman, I presume," he greeted, his voice as smooth as the polished wings of the planes themselves.

Bessie grinned, her dark eyes glinting with the same mixture of curiosity and boldness. "Indeed, you presume correctly," she replied in French, hoping she could converse smoothly with this native Frenchman. "How did you know it was me?"

René gaze slightly softened as he took her in, noting her confident bearing despite the clear and conspicuous distance between her and anyone else around.

"Antoine mentioned that I might be meeting a woman of exceptional beauty today," René said. He gave a respectful dip of his head, a soft smile dancing on his lips. "He didn't lie." René clicked his heels together and bowed slightly, showcasing his courtly French manners. "René Caudron, at your service."

Bessie chuckled, tilting her head in mild amusement. "Are all Frenchmen so skilled at flattery?"

"If only," René replied, a faint twinkle in his eye. "May I show you around? I trust your accommodations in Rouen are suitable?"

"They are, yes—a shared house, clean and compact," Bessie answered. "Comfortable enough."

"Excellent. Come then." With her worry about René understanding her French now dissipated, he gestured toward the buildings clustered ahead like an usher, inviting her to take the lead. Together, they headed toward the wooden schoolhouse nestled among the low buildings of *Le Ecole d'Aviation Caudron.*

Inside, the school felt intimate and functional. The lounge area at the entrance had little more than a few chairs and tables for students to rest between classes. A long hallway ran past a series of empty classrooms with doors left ajar. René pointed out each space as they passed.

"The lounge," he said, nodding to the modest furnishings. "The classrooms. Here, we teach students on the ground before sending them into the air. The lessons must be ingrained in our pilots before they set foot in a cockpit."

René paused and raised his hand as if underscoring a critical point. "It must be solid in your mind before you fly. The noise, vibration, and alien surroundings make learning difficult once you're airborne. Study, then practice." His words hung in the air, heavy with meaning, and Bessie absorbed them in silence.

From the hallway, they entered a hangar, the walls lined with the skeletal frames of Caudron C3 aircraft, each at a different stage of repair or assembly. Mechanics and student pilots worked side by side, lifting panels, tightening bolts, and adjusting ailerons with a determined focus.

"We are hands-on here," René explained, watching her expression closely. "To survive, a pilot must understand mechanics. Is your aircraft fit to fly? That decision is yours alone."

"But if a mechanic says it's safe and in good condition?" Bessie countered with her brow slightly raised.

René's face grew serious. "That is only his opinion. The responsibility, however, rests with the pilot. The pilot must be able to say no." He gave her a pointed look, his words low and measured, their significance clear. "Especially when circumstances are pressing."

Bessie's wide-eyed gaze swept over the workshop's expanse as they moved deeper into the factory. A sea of craftsmen—woodworkers, fabric workers, and fitters—bustled about, meticulously piecing together the fragile bodies of planes. The factory hummed with purpose, its air thick with the scent of varnish and oil.

"Hands-on indeed," she murmured.

René chuckled softly. "Don't let it intimidate you. We're here to teach you to learn. You have time. The course lasts seven months, and by the end, all of this…" He paused as he gestured dramatically around him, then continued. "…will feel as natural as breathing."

They climbed to a hillside that overlooked the Crotoy beach. Below, the sandy expanse stretched wide and smooth in the low tide. Bessie's eyes narrowed as she spotted a squat, awkward aircraft veering down the shoreline, zigzagging clumsily as it ran.

"We call that 'The Penguin,'" René said, his tone laced with fond amusement.

"A fitting name for a bird that can't fly," Bessie remarked dryly.

"Indeed," René laughed. "But you're about to witness a marvel. This particular Penguin can fly—at least, for very short distances anyway."

As they watched, a group of mechanics huddled around the Penguin, making swift adjustments. Moments later, it tore off again, its wheels kicking up a spray of sand before it lifted barely off the ground, gliding a meager fifty yards before it touched back down. René turned to her with one brow raised.

"What do you think?" he asked.

Bessie crossed her arms, a knowing glint in her eye. "You clipped its wings and restricted its power."

René's mouth twitched into a half-smile. "Very perceptive. You'll do well."

As the Penguin taxied back to the line of waiting mechanics, René continued, "When the student can track straight and master these 'crow hops,' they're ready to take up an instructor."

Aerial view of L'ecole Caudron and beach

Bessie and a group of students from the L'ecole Caudron

The Caudron Brothers Biplane

Caudron hydroplane at LeCrotoy Beach

Biplane taking off at Le Crotoy Beach

Caudron hydroplane at LeCrotoy Beach

les ateliers des aéroplanes
à Rue

CA

Caudron Brothers and with their aircraft workers

CHAPTER NINE

Rene

———

Bessie quickly fell into a routine in her aviation school. In the mornings, she joined her fellow students in a small classroom for ground instruction. Guy Perraud, a French instructor with a pronounced limp and a thick, authoritative voice, introduced himself on the first day with dry humor.

"Good morning, future masters of the skies," he greeted them, his cane rhythmically tapping as he made his way to the front of the room. "Or at least, that's my hope. Because, as you'll soon discover, you must be the master of everything— your machine, your course, your circumstances. That is your burden if you wish to roam the skies."

With a thump of his cane, Guy moved closer to the dead center of the room. "Brief introductions are in order. I am Guy Perraud, and yes, I carry a little souvenir from encounters with the Boche."

He nodded towards Bessie to continue the introductions.

"I'm Bessie Coleman from Chicago, Illinois, USA." The introductions continued.

"Albert Berger, from Paris," said a confident, well-dressed twenty-five-year-old young man.

"Charles Durand, late of Cherbourg," said a mustached, twenty-six-year-old, quieter young man.

"Donald Etienne, recently arrived from Brussels," said the last young man, a soft-spoken twenty-three-year-old.

Guy nodded and moved to the chalkboard to outline the upcoming lessons.

"So, we will break down the subjects into knowledge used aloft, aerodynamics, physiology, navigation, etc."

As Guy looked over his shoulder to ensure the students were engaged, he noticed Bessie furiously making notes in her notebook. Guy continued.

"And things of a mechanical nature, engines, structures and such. It is not our intent to make you into mechanics, but intimate knowledge will be most useful."

Every day brought another lesson, each more taxing than the last. Bessie and her classmates donned aprons, sanded wing structures in the factory, and stretched fabric over the frame with the factory workers. At one point, Bessie found herself stitching fabric to a wing with skillful ease while her classmates struggled. She grinned, feeling satisfied with her competence. Every detail—the smell of sawdust, the creak of the factory floor, the echo of hammer on wood—rooted her more profoundly in the journey she had begun.

One rainy afternoon, as she prepared to head home, Bessie was gathering her things when she noticed a car idling beside the school's entrance. René sat inside, looking out at her through the misted window. He motioned for her to join him, and with a small smile, she opened the door and climbed in, grateful for the warmth and the ride.

With a flick of his wrist, René rolled down his window, letting the cold wind rush in. He tossed his cigarette into the night, embers fading like a whisper, and raised the window just as quickly. René tightened his grip on the steering wheel as the car hummed along the rain-soaked, winding road. Droplets slipped down the windshield in streaks, reflecting dim flashes of light from passing lampposts. The world beyond the glass was a mix of shadows, mist, and endless dark forest, yet Bessie sat calmly beside him, peeling off her scarf and folding it with purpose. Now neatly collapsed, her umbrella lay in her lap like a tucked-away promise of shelter. Glancing at Bessie, he couldn't help his curiosity.

"I am curious." His tone held the faintest glint of amusement. "Fourteen kilometers to Rouen, in winter's rain and dark. You intend to walk?"

She tilted her head toward him, her eyes unwavering. "I've walked to and from school my whole life. That is unless I could hitch a ride on a wagon."

René grinned, catching her challenge. "Well, then consider this car a wagon."

"Okay, but the horse is a bit thin," Bessie shot back, eliciting a chuckle from René.

He wasn't entirely sure where this conversation was going but found himself drawn to her spirit. René's curiosity deepened..

"Miss Coleman," he began, a hint of something softer, almost admiring, in his voice, "you intrigue me. I've never met anyone like you."

Her posture shifted, and there was a slight edge in her stance as if preparing for a blow. Bessie's next words were precise and even. "You mean a woman of color?"

René chuckled, shaking his head. "Oh no. Not that at all." He measured his following words, knowing they could either build or break the fragile trust forming between them. "It's your curiosity, your intensity. You take notes, even when others simply listen, yet you don't need those notes, do you?"

Bessie nodded, and René continued. "You pursue preparation at every turn. You live, breathe, and sleep aviation."

She looked straight ahead, the rain-slicked glass reflecting streaks of headlights, shadows of their past travels. "Those notes aren't for today," she admitted, "but for the day I open my own school back in the States."

QUEEN OF THE SKIES

A flicker of pride—admiration—crossed René's face as he turned to her, catching her profile in the dim glow. "I think you're working for more than just a school. It's something more than money, isn't it?"

Her lips pressed together, and a shadow darkened her eyes as they drifted to the stormy scene beyond. "You know how people like me are treated in the States. If I fail, I bring all of them with me. But if I fly..." Her voice trailed off, leaving the words suspended like the tension in the car, tight and full of promise.

René nodded, a simple, weighty gesture. "Then humanity will soar."

The rain had softened to a drizzle as they pulled up in front of her modest house. René parked and climbed out, moving around to open her door. As she stepped out, their eyes met in the dim glow from a streetlamp, the silence between them filling with something unspoken.

René offered a gentle smile. "Safe and sound."

A flicker of something—gratitude, perhaps something more—crossed her face. She stood before him, letting her usual guard down for a moment. "Thank you, Mr. Caudron. I appreciate it."

"Please, call me René," he said, catching her eye. "At school, it's Mr. Caudron. Outside, it's René."

Bessie gave him a rare smile, nodding. "All right, then. Thank you, René." She extended a hand, which he took, his grip firm yet warm. With a slight bow, he brought her hand to his lips for a brief, light kiss.

Bessie's cheeks flushed, her expression a mixture of surprise and amusement as she withdrew her hand. She lingered a moment in his presence before turning and slipping into the house. René stood alone, watching her disappear, and shook his head, a grin still playing at his lips as he closed the door behind her.

PART 4

First to Fly

CHAPTER TEN
At Home in the Clouds

The brisk and unrelenting wind swept over the Crotoy beach, carrying the sharp scent of salt and oil across the stretch of sand that served as Bessie's proving ground. With its taut lines and sleek fuselage, the Penguin sat waiting—a hulking creature that looked more like a mechanical bird grounded on the shore than an aircraft meant to defy gravity.

Bessie sat in the pilot's seat, her shoulders tense as she adjusted the thick leather strap across her chest. Her hands felt the cold metal of the controls, a touchstone of reassurance amid her nerves. Goggles rested on her forehead above her leather flying helmet, yet to be lowered. Beside her, Guy was a steady presence, his eyes sharp and calculating, the weight of experience clear in every word he spoke.

"Alright, as we discussed," he said in a calm voice, edged with a command that broke through the pounding rhythm of her heart. "Focus on the big picture—and on every task you need to complete that picture. Nothing overwhelms. You know this."

Bessie drew a steady breath, nodding. She called out, her voice stronger than she felt.

"Controls checked. Fuel on. Magneto off. Chocks on!" she called.

Her gaze darted to her left and right, catching Charles and Albert's eyes, who waited beside the aircraft's wheels, the ropes in their hands taut and ready. They both gave her a thumbs-up, their faces set in quiet support. The beach felt vast and intimate, a world condensed into the narrow space of sand under the Penguin's wings and the endless sky above.

"Easy, smooth movements," Guy reminded her. "Don't overcontrol. Smooth…"

The mechanic at the propeller called back, steady and sure.

"Chocks on, throttle closed, magneto off."

Bessie's fingers moved over each control, double-checking.

"Closed and off!" she called back.

The mechanic rotated the propeller through five deliberate turns. Each one felt like the drumbeat before a charge. Finally, he called out, "Contact!"

"Contact!" she echoed, her voice carrying across the sand.

The mechanic swung the propeller. The engine caught with a roar, filling the air with the hard-edged sound of power. Bessie watched as Guy gave her a nod and motioned for her to pull down her goggles before turning to hobble out of the way, moving urgently and fighting the unsteady sand beneath his cane. She hesitated, a slight blush touching her cheeks at the reminder, then grinned and lowered them. Charles and Albert pulled the chocks clear of the wheels at the signal, stepping back with quick thumbs-up gestures.

Bessie felt the engine's vibrations travel through the aircraft. She gathered her nerves and eased the throttle forward with her left hand. The Penguin began to roll, cutting through the sand like a knife through rough cloth. The beach and the world around it slipped away, narrowing into the path before her.

As she gained speed, Bessie's feet moved deftly on the rudder bar, feeling the pulse of the aircraft's motion. The Penguin swerved abruptly to the left, then jerked to the right as she corrected. Her pulse raced as the plane veered sharply to the right again. She cut the throttle, but not soon enough to prevent the left wing from dipping precariously toward the sand.

The Penguin jolted to a stop, resting at a tilted angle. For a moment, she only heard the engine's tick-tick-tick as it settled, the sound echoing in the sudden silence. Her heart still pounded as a reminder of how close she'd come to losing control.

Up the beach, she caught sight of Guy's raised hand, holding back Albert, who had already taken a step toward her. They waited, watching, two hundred yards away, giving her space to make the next move.

She took a long breath, steeling herself. Her hands tightened around the controls. Checking her position, she braced her feet, touched the throttle, and slowly added power. With measured precision, she coaxed the Penguin back to its starting point, aligning it again with the narrow path in front of her.

"I'm not giving up," she whispered to herself.

Bessie kept her eyes forward as she accelerated the aircraft. Her pulse quickened as she skillfully maneuvered the plane a complete one hundred eighty degrees, her mission completed. Bessie grinned from ear to ear as her classmates came running towards her, whooping in triumph for her success. Bessie laughed at their elation, then realized she had to get out of the cockpit to give one of them a turn. She realized she didn't want to. She finally felt like a professional pilot.

The following days of training were exhilarating and challenging. The letter Bessie wrote to her family was euphoric.

"Dear Momma, I'm flying now!" Susan said as she read Bessie's most recent letter aloud to the children. "I've been in the cockpit three times, and I'm getting off the ground. It's scary but fun. I've got to practice a lot before I can fly alone, but I'm on my way!"

John, who had been in the room to hear the letter too, smiled knowingly at Momma, who returned his glance. While Bessie was learning to fly, Momma's reading improved daily.

Then came the day that started as usual, with a charged breeze rustling the coast. Bessie's classmate, Charles, took to the air in his Caudron G3. He flew out over the water at a steady four hundred feet, his smile wide with confidence, a rush of wind against his face. In a smooth motion, he began a turn, banking left, angling down towards the beach.

From below, Guy, Albert, and Donald followed Charles's flight with awe. Then suddenly, the Caudron's bank increased sharply, the nose dipping too low. Guy tensed. His eyes were fixed on the plane.

"Level!" he shouted, his voice roaring through the air, hoping to reach Charles' ears. "Level the damn wings!"

As the aircraft's wings angled nearly perpendicular to the ground, the plane seemed to fight Charles's controls, its roll hesitating before reversing slowly. Guy's voice grew even sharper, his urgency evident.

"Level, then pull! Level!" he screamed.

Inside the cockpit, Charles, panic evident in his eyes, yanked the control stick hard to the right. He pulled back desperately, but it was too late. The ground rushed toward him in a dizzying blur. The plane snapped in a hard right roll, colliding with the beach in a shuddering impact.

Guy, leaning heavily on his cane, broke into an uneven sprint toward the wreckage, a hundred yards across the sand. Bessie and Albert reached Charles first, tearing frantically at the fuselage's torn fabric as the smell of leaking fuel filled the air. Guy pried away splintered wooden struts with his cane. Meanwhile, the mechanics sped down the beach, clutching a stretcher. Together, they managed to pull Charles free, but he lay bloodied, unresponsive. They checked him for a pulse, then watched as the emergency medical team lifted Charles's body onto the stretcher and into the ambulance. Bessie's throat caught a large sob, and Albert, who was standing next to her, instantly enfolded her into a hug. She could feel the sorrow in his chest. She saw Guy shake his head slowly, eyes to the ground. Every pilot there was tragically reminded of the dangers that shadowed every flight. Yet even as the ambulance doors closed, as a wave of grief swept over her and her thoughts turned to what this meant for her aviation career, she felt the burn of determination within her. Despite the risks, she decided this path wasn't one she could leave now.

****

The accident was not discussed, nor forgotten. After Charles's memorial service, the students had an unwritten rule not to raise the topic, but Bessie overheard two instructors discussing it in hushed whispers as she came around a corner in the hallway the next day. She had faith in her instructors and knew that a student's demise must weigh heavily on them. She remembered what René said about pilots taking responsibility for their own flights. It involved assuming risk, too, which could be lowered considerably with the proper training and preparation to prevent danger and safely land the plane in any circumstance.

Several days later, Bessie was on the same beach, ready for her solo test. She was seated solidly in the Cauldron G3. Her instructor, Vincent Faix, stood beside her. He was a tall, thin, elegant man.

"It's time. I couldn't have done that better myself—three takeoffs and landings," Vincent said, smiling. "Enjoy it!"

Steadily, Bessie lifted off, circling above the beach. From the ground, René and Vincent watched her glide through the air.

"She looks steady," René noted, with admiration in his voice.

Vincent nodded. "Very. That young lady is one of the best students I've had. What drives her so?"

"There's more on those shoulders than you could ever imagine," René said, his tone softened with respect. "She succeeds, and a great many lives change for the better."

Above, Bessie maneuvered the Cauldron with skill and grace, alongside confidence built and reinforced from her previous flights. She touched down, lifted off again, and finally rolled to a smooth stop near Vincent and René. Bessie climbed out of the cockpit. Her face was radiant with achievement. She ran over to hug Vincent and René, laughing with pure joy.

The next day, Guy held a class on navigation, guiding the students through the logistics of a flight path they would soon all navigate independently. Bessie, Donald, and Albert sat at their desks with navigational charts, compass dividers, note paper, and pencils, rapt with attention on their instructor.

"Today, you brush the dust off your navigation classwork, for tomorrow, you'll put it to the test," he said. Guy walked over to the blackboard and wrote down the weather reports for Le Crotoy, Dieppe, and Melleville airfields. "Please plan a flight with stops at these airfields, with a return to Le Crotoy."

Bessie sat up in her chair. She had already planned cross-country flights and flown them with instructors. Now it was time for her to plan and make a cross-country flight alone.

"Tomorrow, we expect you to act independently," Vincent said, confirming Bessie's thoughts. "You command the flight. We will give no feedback."

"If you have questions, just ask. We will be around to check your work, but tomorrow you will check it for real," said Guy.

Bessie charted her course meticulously, noting every airfield, milestone, and estimated flight time. She was ready to prove herself in the air and against the map, flying alone and responsible for every choice in the cockpit.

The following day, Bessie flew the Caudron G3 over a patchwork of forests and fields in the beautiful French countryside. Every passing town and landmark was a calculated milestone on her journey as she piloted the aircraft over lush green forests and brown fields parallel to the shoreline. She was southeast bound at three thousand feet altitude. Bessie glanced at her watch and noted the time on passing Mers-les-Bains off the aircraft's right side. She compared the aircraft compass against the flight log with satisfaction. Soon, she was passing her next landmark, the town of Petit Caux. Whenever she grew uncertain, she checked her watch, recalculated her position, and pressed on as she navigated toward Dieppe airfield.

As Bessie completed her test flight and returned to Le Crotoy, she circled low over the landmarks, each maneuver underscoring her mastery of the skies. She cut the engine and landed precisely, stopping her plane in perfect alignment on the marked line in the sand. The crowd on the beach erupted with applause. Caudron employees, students, instructors, and even officials pressed in, shaking her hand, offering congratulations, and showering her with the accolades she had rightly earned.

Vincent greeted her as she touched down on the beach. "Once more, blind luck and superstition have won out over skill and science," he teased.

Grinning, Bessie quipped back, "I think superior instruction may have played a part as well."

Soon, news of her achievement traveled across the oceans in a chorus of Morse code messages to newsrooms worldwide. Bessie Coleman had earned her Federation *Aéronautique Internationale* pilot's license and was the first black woman to do so.

Later that evening, René drove her to Rouen, where they walked together through the city square. The statue of Joan of Arc, hero and martyr, stood illuminated in the evening light, emitting strength and beauty in its soft glow.

René turned to her. "You see, you are not the first young lady to grace this city on a quest to free her people," he said with a warm smile. "She, like you, found her way here by chance. And like you, she was slated to do great things."

Bessie gazed up at the monument, her mind heavy with thoughts of her journey. "Different times, different people," she replied thoughtfully.

René nodded. "True. For her, it was the British. For you, it is human ignorance. I'd hate to guess which is a tougher enemy."

"But against all odds, she vanquished the English," Bessie countered. "Perhaps I have a chance after all."

As the evening ended and they reached her doorway, Bessie turned to René. "Tomorrow it's off to Paris, then Cherbourg."

"Then on to home," René said with a hint of sadness. "A lot of work ahead, no?"

"Been working all my life," she replied, her gaze unfaltering. "If I stop, I don't know what'll happen."

"So, are you happy?" René asked hesitantly.

"Happy, scared, a little of both."

"Plot your course. Maintain awareness and control. You'll do fine."

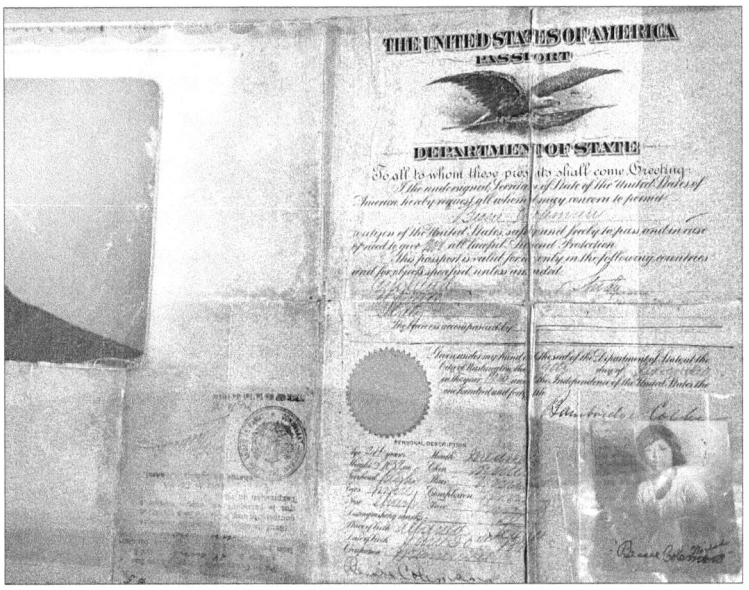

Bessie's US Passport

Bessie's aviation license from the Fédération Aéronautique Internationale

CHAPTER ELEVEN

Home Sweet Home

On September 29, 1921, the SS Manchuria rocked gently beside the dock, a hulking iron beast that had crossed oceans with tireless resilience. The city knew that the vessel carried a special cargo—Bessie Coleman. A faint drizzle hung in the air, coating the scene in a silvery haze as passengers disembarked, stepping into the buzz of New York City with relief and wonder. Among them, Bessie appeared on the gangway, stepping down with purposeful strides. She held her head high, and her sharp eyes missed nothing as she looked over the unfamiliar landscape ahead.

Almost immediately, she was swallowed by a swarm of reporters. Cameras flashed, capturing her in that moment, newly returned from Europe. She was a woman of firsts. As questions fired from every direction, she turned, meeting each gaze squarely with a calm confidence that silenced the crowd, if only for a beat.

"Miss Coleman, how does it feel to have been awarded your piloting license?" a reporter from the *New York Times*, with a booming voice, asked above the noise of the crowd.

Bessie's lips curved in a faint, patient smile. "My license was earned, not awarded," she said, her voice clear and firm. "Earned through hard work and skill, just like any other pilot in the world."

More questions followed, tumbling one over another, each voice more desperate than the last.

QUEEN OF THE SKIES

"What are your ambitions now that you're back?" asked a reporter from the *Detroit Free Press*. A pause hung in the air as the crowd held its breath.

"Of course, I'll be visiting family," Bessie said, the faintest edge of warmth in her tone, "but my ambition is to open a flight school."

The *Los Angeles Examiner* reporter shouted from the back, "Where and when will you open it?"

Bessie's gaze drifted over the crowd as if she could see her dreams taking shape there among them. She felt the weight of her words as she spoke. "There are many details to work out," she replied, "but with any luck, we'll have it up and running within the year. The location has yet to be determined."

Another question shot up from the fray. "Will it be just for people of color? Where will your instructors come from?"

"The school will be open to anyone who wants to learn to fly, regardless of their color or sex," she replied, her eyes flashing. "There are countless eligible instructor pilots available."

Around her, the murmurs grew as more questions launched from the crowd, voices thick with curiosity and a touch of disbelief. Bessie didn't flinch. Each question came like a small wave, which she met with unwavering poise.

"Do you have aircraft?" the *Detroit Free Press* reporter asked.

"All in good time," Bessie replied with a patient grin. "I've barely gotten back. There are many, many aircraft readily available."

"How did you find you find the people in France?"

A photographer positioned his camera for a perfect shot. Bessie paused, looked directly at the lens, and murmured in her steady, measured French, *"Ils sont vraiment un peuple beau, patient, et intelligent."*

"And what does that mean, Miss Coleman?" the photographer asked.

"They are truly a beautiful, patient, and intelligent people," Bessie replied, flickers of her instructors flashing through her mind, "They never treated me differently because of the color of my skin."

The cameras clicked, and her image was captured. Her gaze was bold, a vision of hope and defiance. The New York Times reporter leaned forward with bright eyes.

"Will you be staying in New York long?"

Bessie glanced his way, taking a measured breath. "I have some speaking engagements before I return to Chicago."

Another reporter, this time from the Los Angeles Examiner, raised his voice above the murmur. "Why did you take up flying?"

Her gaze settled on him, and her answer cut through the crowd, calm and resolute. "Aviation is the future, and people of the race need to be part of that future. We cannot settle for being told we aren't capable or left behind."

A flicker of intensity sparked in her gaze. "If we accept limitations others impose—or those we impose on ourselves—then indeed, those are our limits."

Bessie graciously excused herself from the reporters who followed her, shouting questions as she made her way to the street and into a waiting taxi. She shut the door on the din and asked the driver to take her directly to the Metropolitan Baptist Church in Manhattan.

When Bessie arrived, she could see the throng of parishioners, reporters, and guests in attendance to hear her speak. There was an electric energy in the air, and faces glowed with anticipation. She looked around, and her eyes rested on Alderman George Harris, who had been heading her way to greet her, but now motioned her to the front of the church, near the podium, where he was standing. Once united, he greeted her warmly and then loudly asked the people to quiet down. The rows of children sitting front and center were wide-eyed and snapped to attention at his request. Bessie could see that people occupied every available seat in the church.

"We have the great honor and privilege to welcome Miss Bessie Coleman," Harris began, his voice clear and proud. "An intrepid colored woman, a pioneering woman, a great American."

He paused, lifting a handkerchief to his brow as the crowded room fell silent in expectation. "Bessie journeyed thousands of miles across that great ocean, alone, determined to learn to fly." The reverend paused again, a glint of admiration in his eyes as he raised his voice to add, "To fly!"

A wave of applause rose from the crowd. The Alderman swept his gaze over the audience before gesturing toward Bessie.

"Not only did she succeed, but she also received an international flying license—a feat only a few in the world— male, female, white, or colored—have ever achieved. On top of that, she has been admitted into the prestigious Aero Club of France. Please extend a warm welcome to an extraordinary individual, Miss Bessie Coleman."

The applause rose to a roar. Bessie made her way to the pulpit, smiling. Her gaze settled on the rows of young faces in front.

"Thank you, Brother Harris," she said, her voice carrying a deep sense of conviction. "Glory be unto God, for through Him all things are possible." Harris nodded in agreement, his expression mirroring the audience's admiration. She let the room settle before she continued, her voice gentle yet steady.

"Thank you, everyone, for being here today," she began.

"Normally, I would enthrall you with flowery descriptions of the joy and freedom of flight, but I'd like to take a break from that speech to address the children, our collective future."

She paused, letting her gaze fall on the children in the front rows. A flicker of delight ran through the youngsters as Bessie continued.

"In the country of India, they have elephants. Mighty giants, wondrous creatures, tall and strong. But when they're young, to control them, their masters put a shackle around one of their hind legs, attaching it with a short length of chain to a tiny tent peg in the ground. As a baby, that peg holds the elephant in place. But the elephant grows. They stand twelve feet tall and weigh thousands of pounds."

She paused, glancing down at the rapt expressions on the children's faces. "And even then, even when they're that big, that little peg, now barely a toothpick to that magnificent beast, still holds them in place. Why?" she asked, her voice a quiet but powerful challenge. The children murmured, whispering guesses amongst themselves, their curiosity piqued.

"Because that's all they know. If they're attached to that little piece of wood, they think they can't go anywhere." She let her words resonate, knowing the message was sinking in. She could see understanding beginning to dawn on young faces.

"A fully grown elephant could pull up that peg like it wasn't even there," she continued, her voice a steady reminder of the strength they all carried. "But in his mind, he's helpless."

Bessie smiled at the children. "Look at you here today. The next generation is on the cusp of breaking free. The only thing holding you back are the puny limitations in our minds."

The church erupted in applause, loud and heartfelt as ever been. Bessie had moved the crowd with her message of resilience and determination. As she settled into the taxi for her next and most important stop, she breathed a sigh of relief. After all these years, she was coming home.

There were tears, hugs, and more tears as Bessie entered the apartment. Momma clutched her like she wouldn't let go, and even her big brothers were hanging on Bessie's every word as she answered all their questions about learning to fly. A feeling of warmth and comfort flooded Bessie as she looked around at the faces of those who loved and knew her best.

"How long do we have you for?" Momma asked anxiously.

"Probably not long, Momma," Bessie replied. "I have a lot to do."

SS Manchuria circa 1920s.

CHAPTER TWELVE

Aerobatics in Europe

R obert Abbott's office was a study in subdued elegance. The midday sun cast streaks of gold onto the polished mahogany desk. Behind it, Robert leaned back in his chair, a faint air of authority softened by his ever-present warmth. Jessie sat beside him, his posture poised, while David Behncke, a man whose presence seemed to fill the room, occupied the chair closest to Bessie.

David Behncke had the build of someone who lived purposely—broad shoulders, a muscular frame, and a mustache that framed a face weathered by wind and altitude. His handshake was firm, almost challenging, but his eyes held a glint of humor as he addressed Bessie.

"Bessie," Robert began evenly, though his pride was evident, "I'd like to introduce my friend David, David Behncke."

David leaned forward, offering his hand. "A pleasure to meet you," he said, his voice smooth, with just a hint of gravel.

Bessie returned the handshake, matching his firmness. "The pleasure's mine."

Jessie chimed in, her tone light but precise. "Mr. Behncke owns Checkerboard Airport. He was flying for the army until recently."

David chuckled softly at the introduction, the sound resonating like a low engine hum.

"David knows a few things about making a buck with airplanes," Robert added, a playful grin tugging at the corners of his mouth.

"More than a few," David interjected, his smile widening. "I dabble in airshow promotion and represent a fair amount of talent on that circuit."

Bessie tilted her head slightly, her curiosity piqued. "So you're a booking agent?"

"More of a talent agent with connections," David corrected. "But I still do a bit of flying myself, in addition to running Checkerboard."

Jessie leaned forward, his enthusiasm unmistakable. "Bess, David knows what's happening in aviation, especially aerial expositions."

David shifted his gaze back to Bessie, his expression sobering. "The flat truth is, there aren't many jobs out there for someone who just wants to fly. And for a woman of color?" He paused, letting the weight of his words settle. "Even fewer."

Bessie's spine stiffened. Her jaw tightened, but her eyes stayed locked on David. Robert's reassuring glance caught hers, silently urging patience.

"Well," Bessie said evenly, her voice carrying a quiet strength, "if you're trying to talk me out of flying, you're about two years too late. But something tells me you didn't come here to convince these gentlemen to see me quit."

David inclined his head, a gesture of respect. "Hardly. But a lot's changed since you left for France. Just flying won't cut it anymore—not for a paying crowd."

Bessie's features softened, curiosity replacing her initial defensiveness.

David leaned back slightly, his hands resting on the armrests of his chair. "Two months ago, Laura Brownell did one hundred ninety-nine consecutive loops. And Lillian Boyer? She's out there barnstorming, jumping mid-air from one plane to another."

Bessie's eyebrows rose, her skepticism giving way to reluctant understanding.

"So you think I need to be barnstorming?" she asked.

"Not barnstorming," David replied firmly. "Flying out of hayfields is a great way to starve. I'm talking about organized expositions—thousands of tickets sold at once. And ride hopping on top of that. With the right management, you could make real money. So, tell me, Bessie. How good are you at acrobatics?"

Bessie let out a low chuckle. "If I tried those stunts down low, Mr. Abbott here would be printing my obituary within a day or two."

The room broke into light laughter, a momentary easing of tension. Then Bessie spoke.

"Like I said," Bessie interjected defiantly, "nobody here better be talking about me quitting."

Robert raised a hand, his expression a blend of reassurance and determination. Switching to French, he spoke softly to give his words extra weight. I think you need to return to school."

David leaned forward again, his voice measured. "At Robert and Jessie's urging, I've reached out to some instructors in Europe. They specialize in what they call 'Flying of the Arts'."

Bessie's face lit up for the first time in the conversation--not with defiance, but with genuine surprise. Possibility shimmered in the air, a chance to rewrite her story on her terms.

****

The sleek black car hummed softly over the narrow, tree-lined road leading out of Veere, Netherlands. It seemed to glide under the steady hands of the chauffeur, Anthony Fokker, a dark-haired, clean-shaven man in his mid-thirties. He maintained a disciplined rhythm as the wheels rolled across the gravel. Seated beside her was Alfred Keller, also in his mid-thirties with a gentlemanly mustache, who spoke with a thick German accent.

Anthony leaned slightly forward, his eyes bright with the satisfaction of a man who had rebuilt himself and his empire from the ashes of war. His dark, slicked-back hair lent him an air of meticulous control, though a tiny glint of impatience edged his tone as he spoke.

"We're almost there," Anthony announced, his voice threaded with restrained pride. "We have so much to teach you, Bessie. Besides learning acrobatics, you'll find that we've been quite busy with the unpleasantness of the war behind us."

Alfred gave a small, approving nod. He always carried himself with a disciplined formality.

"Most of the designs are for transport planes," he added, glancing at the landscape that had seen the effects of war firsthand. "There's a growing interest for them in civil and military markets."

Bessie's attention snapped to Alfred, intrigued. Her brows rose, a spark of excitement in her eyes.

"When you say transports, how many seats, what kind of wingspan?" she asked. She knew that the capabilities of modern aircraft were changing faster than anyone could keep up with. Anthony responded without hesitation, leaning toward her.

"We are currently working on twelve seats with a span of some twenty meters," he said.

"It's got an American Liberty engine," Alfred interjected,

pride lacing his voice. "One of the big ones. Four hundred horsepower."

Bessie's lips parted slightly, impressed despite herself. A craft that size and power could take commercial aviation into a new era.

"Has she flown yet?" she asked, turning to Anthony.

He shook his head, a glimmer of anticipation in his eyes. "No, but very soon. We'll tour the factory, and then you and Roland can exercise some of the toys."

She nodded, already feeling the excitement tightening in her chest. At the Fokker factory, the factory floor stretched out like a mechanical forest before Bessie, with skeletal metal frames and freshly painted fuselages scattered about, waiting to be assembled into functional aircraft. Bessie moved among them, absorbing the hum of industry and catching close-up glimpses of the skilled hands at work. Workers carefully maneuvered parts with precision, fitting wings to fuselages and securing engines under the strict gaze of foremen who prowled the aisles, keen-eyed and diligent.

Anthony and Alfred accompanied her, pointing out areas of interest with evident pride. Bessie focused intensely on the intricate assembly, the way each piece seemed to find its place as though by some hidden logic only the workers understood. She leaned in closer to inspect the details, her fingers itching to touch the machines, to understand their mechanics. Meanwhile, Anthony and Alfred exchanged looks of admiration and surprise, noting her intense interest in the construction of each aircraft. She seemed to know exactly where to look and what questions to ask. Here was someone who truly understood the machinery before her.

Once in the cockpit of the Fokker DIII, the aircraft hummed smoothly under Bessie's skilled touch. She felt the power of the Liberty engine resonating through her hands as she held the controls, guiding the plane over the pastoral Dutch landscape. Windmills dotted the countryside below, their blades turning steadily as they cruised over the fields.

From the front seat, Alfred leaned back and pointed down to one of the clusters of windmills. With a subtle hand signal, he told Bessie to descend and bank toward the landmark. Bessie responded by tipping the aircraft into a descending turn. The DIII responded like an extension of her own will as they circled over the landscape. They swept across the fields in a low arc, dipping near enough to send the soft drone of its engine echoing through the rows of windmills. Bessie's heart quickened as the land rushed up, only to fall away again as they ascended once more, the wheels barely grazing the air above the crop tops. She couldn't help but smile as they leveled out, her hands steady, her eyes gleaming with the thrill of it. Alfred was also grinning, their silent understanding cemented by the shared joy of flight.

Later, from the ground, Alfred and Anthony watched Bessie fly the DII alone from the Fokker factory's hangar ramp. It was an endless expanse of cement and steel that held the promise of adventure. The biplane arced gracefully into the air, then pitched sharply upward, engine roaring as it looped against the backdrop of Veere's open skies. Alfred's watchful gaze followed the plane's flawless trajectory, his eyes narrowing with appreciation.

"A natural, Tony. Smooth. Flies beyond her hours. I think the acrobatics will go well," he murmured, folding his arms.

"Well, that sounds like what David said to expect. What time do you two start in the morning?" Anthony replied, observing the plane's movement with a satisfied grin. "Looks like she enjoys it."

Alfred nodded. His admiration was palpable. "Yes. But not so much as to be distracted."

Later, Alfred accompanied Bessie in the air again in a two-seat Fokker. He signaled Bessie to fly a hammerhead turn from the front cockpit. Bessie thrust the biplane skyward on a vertical line of flight, then slowed it to pivot, diving vertically. She tilted her head back, smiling as she pulled out of the dive. Alfred pumped his fist in triumph, then signaled her to roll the aircraft. Bessie did a perfect four-point roll and was pleased with the aircraft's smooth handling. As the Fokker biplane finally landed from its aeronautic adventures, Anthony walked up to the pair as they climbed down from the aircraft.

"One of your better students, I dare say," Anthony said to Alfred with a grin.

The trio retreated into the Fokker office, and Anthony leaned casually against the corner of his polished desk, studying Bessie. She sat across from him on the couch, unable to read his face but knowing she had done well in his eyes.

"You've impressed Alfred. Nothing but glowing reports," he said. His smile widened as he looked at her. "And not just in how you handle the maneuvers."

Bessie shifted slightly. Her gaze was direct but guarded. "Thank you," she replied, her voice steady. "I appreciate that."

Anthony's expression grew more serious as he leaned in, lowering his voice as if confiding something personal. "He says you're thorough, always prepared, ahead of the aircraft." He paused, watching her reaction. "So, I'll finally get to the point. I'm short a test pilot. The job is yours if you want it."

A spark of joy lit her face, but she contained it quickly, her voice filled with a controlled excitement. "I don't know what to say beyond an emphatic yes," she said.

****

Bessie's starched, patriotic pilot's uniform caught the sunlight, gleaming against the polished chrome of a luxury car. She stood tall on the running board, addressing a small huddle of reporters. She had a steady determination in her stance as she answered their questions. Glenn Curtiss Airfield stretched out in front of her, with a banner behind her reading "Honoring 15th Infantry Regiment" hung from an archway, proudly framing the entrance. Black veterans, many from Long Island or nearby New York City, passed by in uniform, saluting and nodding in quiet respect as they entered the showgrounds.

Robert Abbott and Jessie Binga watched from the edge of the press throng. A New York Times reporter spoke up, pushing his notepad forward as he called out.

"Miss Coleman, three months in Europe—what were you doing there?"

"Well, I was refining my acrobatic flying and later working as a test pilot for the Fokker aircraft company," she said.

"When you say refining, what does that mean?" asked the *Los Angeles Examiner's* reporter, leaning forward.

"I could avail myself of some of the most renowned aces from the Great War. French, German, Dutch—I flew with them and learned their techniques."

A reporter from *The Defender* held her gaze. "Any plans for the future?"

Her expression softened slightly. "Mr. Anthony Fokker is considering opening a factory here in the States. With that will come a flight school open to anyone, regardless of gender or race."

Robert's head turned sharply toward Jessie. An eyebrow arched in intrigue. Jessie let out a low chuckle. "I think she's learning your promotion game, Robert."

"Will you be flying your own airplane here today?" asked the *Los Angeles Examiner.*

"Ah no, not today," replied Bessie, "but I've arranged to use a plane from the Curtiss company. We're in negotiations with Fokker for several for the flight school."

"Well, if you can't envision something, you'll never realize it," Robert told Jessie playfully.

Bessie standing on airplane wheel

David Behnecke, ALPA (Airline Pilot Association) Founder and First President

Anthony Fokker, prominent aviator and leader in aircraft design and manufacture

PART 5

Courage in the Storm

CHAPTER THIRTEEN

Showtime

Bessie strode confidently toward a waiting Curtiss aircraft at the center of Glenn Curtiss Field, her hand raised in a spirited wave to the applauding crowd. The strains of "The Star-Spangled Banner" filled the air as the Fifteenth Regiment Band passed in review, their polished brass instruments gleaming in the bright afternoon sunlight. All around her, an excited crowd of men, women, and children of all races pointed and cheered unabashedly as the announcer's voice crackled a welcome and a glowing introduction of Bessie Coleman over the loudspeakers.

Soon, Bessie and the Curtiss were flying high above the crowd. Spectators lifted their hands to their eyes to block out the bright sun and better see her airplane. The announcer's voice was dramatic and engaging as he narrated the importance of aerobatics during the war.

"Just like our boys did over France to chase down the Hun!" the announcer's voice boomed as Bessie dipped her plane low. She executed a flawless series of rolls that sent gasps rippling through the audience. Every eye followed the aircraft as it twisted and looped through the sky, leaving snake-like airshow smoke in its wake.

"Sometimes, the quickest way to get on the tail of a German was to loop back on them," the announcer's voice rang out again, filling the air with the thrill of suspense.

Bessie's next maneuver—a four-point roll—brought the crowd to its feet, applause and cheers rising to a crescendo. A moment of hushed silence fell as she executed a tight loop, followed by a slow climb to altitude, where she poised the plane for a breathtaking multi-turn spin. The crowd watched in awe as she dove toward the earth, the aircraft spinning like a corkscrew before she leveled it out just above the ground.

"Now there's a demonstration of courage and precision!" the announcer proclaimed.

The crowd applauded enthusiastically as Bessie's aircraft ascended once more. She performed a perfect half loop with rolls that climbed higher into the sky, mesmerizing the spectators below.

"Now Bessie Coleman, "Queen Bess, Queen of the Skies" climbs to display a death-defying multiturn spin," said the announcer.

From her dizzying height, Bess suddenly dove nose first towards the earth. The crowd gasped as they beheld the exciting yet horrifying spectacle. Bess' aircraft gained speed, and just when it seemed she had lost all control and would crash, she pulled out of the spin and leveled the plane. Robert and Jess, who had been holding their breath along with the crowd, smiled at each other in relief. Jessie slapped Robert on the back playfully. Nobody could hold a crowd like Bessie could!

Bessie came to a soft-landing center stage of the crowd. As she stood up in her cockpit and waved energetically at the crowd, they replied with thunderous applause and cheers. The Fifteenth Battalion band marched onto the airfield in prim, uniform lines playing patriotic music, and Bessie's heart swelled with the music.

****

The sun dipped low over the Chicago skyline as Robert sat at his desk, gazing thoughtfully at Bessie. David Behncke sat nearby. His hands gestured wildly as he recounted the past weeks. He was a man of considerable presence with the air of someone who had served in the military. Tall, dark, with a carefully groomed mustache, David was a match for Bessie in many ways. He was an intelligent man of strong will and an accomplished pilot, having served in the Army several times before becoming a show promoter. Now, Bessie had become one of his most lucrative clients, even though her similar intelligence and strong will had her thoroughly questioning bookings before accepting them.

"Two shows already. New York and Memphis. Great crowds at both." He gestured to Bessie. "Your name is not only known but proving to be a draw."

Bessie smiled, remembering a copy of The Defender Susan clipped as a memento of her triumph. The headline read, "Colored Aviatrix Thrills Crowds from New York to Tennessee." She was glad to make her family proud.

"And the ride hopping," Bessie added. "I think I gave twenty or more rides at both shows. Even white folk were riding with me."

Robert leaned forward at his desk, a conspiratorial twinkle in his eye.

"David, why don't you tell her about what else you've got her into?"

"Into?" Bessie asked tentatively.

"Well, you know we've got Checkerboard coming up," said David, speaking of an upcoming air show at the airport he managed outside Chicago. "But I'm thinking of ....California."

Bessie let out a surprised little laugh. "What's in California?"

"They call it the Golden State," replied David. "Hopefully, we'll find some golden opportunities. Build your name. You know, either flying or in the movies."

"Flying, movies?" Bessie replied, shifting in her chair. "What movies are you talking about? Stunt flying in a movie?"

"Not exactly. A movie about you. Your life story."

Bessie gasped inaudibly. "A movie about me. My life?"

"That's what they say," nodded David with a little smile. "We've got a contract to sign and, oh yeah. Coast Tire and Rubber would like you to drop leaflets over Los Angeles for them."

Now, Bessie was beginning to see the cracks in the façade of this suggested adventure. "A leaflet drop? All the way to California to drop handbills?"

"Well, that and an airshow in Palomar Park. Grand opening of the fairgrounds there."

Bessie smiled good-naturedly, recognizing David's tactics to manipulate her without malice. He knew how much she loved playing airshows.

"I'm starting to think this having an agent and not landing in hay fields is going to pay off," she said.

A few days later, Bessie gave the people of Mayfield, Illinois, an exciting aviation show at Checkerboard Field, which would one day be known as Chicago's Midway Airport. She was greeted with a marching band, color guard, and the unbridled cheers of a tremendous mixed-race crowd. Bessie's loops, rolls, and spins mesmerized everyone. The crowd lifted their eyes to the sky in awe of the graceful machine swooping through the air. Bessie also transported a skydiver who jumped from the wing of her plane with breathtaking skill. As the show ended, she landed smoothly onto the runway to the sounds of her adoring fans. As she taxied in, she passed David in another plane, who was giving hopping rides that afternoon and had a white man in the passenger seat. He smiled and gave her a thumbs up, which Bessie returned with a wave.

Bessie felt gratified to see the queue for her hopping rides was long and included both black and white passengers. The smiles of the children there that day warmed her heart as she passed out toy pilot wings to those in attendance. She hoped each one would someday learn to fly.

CHAPTER FOURTEEN

Turning Points

———

The early afternoon sun burned into the metal plaque mounted proudly on the wall, emblazoned with the name "Seminole Film Making Company." Inside the office, gleaning mahogany-paneled walls echoed whispers of old Hollywood. Framed headshots of black actors, each solemn and striking, adorned the room, surrounded by posters that declared "Race Movies" in bold, unapologetic letters. Every corner of the office was clearly designed to project an image of success, of power. Thomas Barker sat at the desk, a black man in his fifties with salt-and-pepper hair and the watchful gaze of someone used to holding power. He wore a tailored suit that almost hid the weight of his years and overeating while making hard decisions.

Next to him, James Fisk stood as a picture of impeccable professionalism, with a thin mustache, slicked hair, and a quiet confidence laced with ambition. He was Barker's right hand, perhaps more calculating than his boss, and equally invested in the success of every studio venture.

Bessie sat across from them, dressed in a sleek, colorful pantsuit that commanded attention. She was reading a script with a blank expression on her face. Fisk and Barker exchanged glances, unable to tell what Bessie was thinking. After a long pause, she calmly looked up at the two men and silently shook her head slowly and deliberately.

She looked back up at the men before reading the script verbatim. "'Bessie, barefoot in a torn dress, walks the streets of New York City.'" She met Barker's eyes evenly. "You forgot the pole with a kerchief full of food tied at the end."

Thomas shifted in his chair, crossing his hands atop the desk, his face a blend of confusion and forced patience. "You have a problem with the character as portrayed, Miss Coleman?"

Bessie sighed and shook her head again, this time to herself. "Let me ask you something, Mr. Thomas Barker. Do you have a sister?"

Thomas seemed taken aback but nodded cautiously. "Yes, as a matter of fact, I do."

Bessie's words became sharper, a scalpel cutting to the quick. "And has she been blessed with children?"

Thomas's hesitation was palpable as he nodded again, the question's intent dawning on him. A small smile crept over Bessie's face. "Then I suppose it's easy for you to decide to be an Uncle Tom, but I won't."

Before Thomas could react, Fisk interjected, his voice steady but with an edge of irritation. "Miss Coleman, this is the script for *Sunshine and Shadow*, and your signature is on a contract saying you're starring in this film."

Bessie straightened, not missing a beat. "What you don't understand, Mr. Fisk, is my life's ambition is to turn *Uncle Tom's Cabin* into a hangar for my airplane," she replied calmly.

With a decisive move, she stood, adjusting her suit jacket with a finality that even the plush, overstuffed office couldn't dampen. Thomas was caught off guard and watched her carefully.

"Miss Coleman, we control the production," Thomas insisted, his voice rising in frustration. "You're under contract. We have a hundred people waiting on set for you."

Bessie set the script down on Barker's desk. "Well, I hope they're good at waiting," she replied cooly. "I've worked my whole life to overcome these stereotypes. I'm not going to stop now."

"Miss Coleman, we can sue you," said James in a warning tone as she proceeded to the door.

Bessie turned to face him. "Go ahead," she replied. "You won't get much," she laughed. Then she walked out the door but turned back to the gentlemen to leave them with one last thought. "Honestly, gentlemen, I'm so disappointed," she said seriously. "It's bad enough when white folk throw this kind of ignorance our way. What's your excuse?"

She closed the door behind her, leaving Thomas and Fisk exchanging helpless, frustrated glances, one silent question hanging between them. Thomas closed his eyes briefly, shaking his head in resignation.

****

The air at Santa Monica's Rockwell Surplus Yard buzzed with the clink of metallic wrenches and the rhythmic hum of machinery. Dust-coated rows of stacked crates with faded military insignias were barely visible under the layers of grime and time. Mechanics in oil-streaked overalls tinkered with the scattered aircraft parts, while others assembled entire planes from salvage lying on the ground.

Bessie stepped confidently into the yard, surveying the mess of metal, dust, and disarray with a discerning eye. Nearby, Vernon Gatis, a gruff, white, grizzled man in dirty overalls, chewed on a wad of tobacco. His gaze narrowed as he noticed her approach. They both stopped before three dilapidated JN-4 "Jenny" aircraft, each looking less airworthy than their neighbor. Vernon spat a tobacco streak onto the ground, wiping his mouth with the back of his hand.

"Them's complete," he grunted. "Engines have been run. First two, anyway." He squinted at her. "Four hundred dollars, cash on the barrelhead."

Bessie gave a curt nod and inspected the planes with a seasoned eye, catching the faint scent of fuel and metal that clung to them.

"Kinda rough," she declared. "Any records with them?"

Vernon let out a short, dry laugh, shaking his head. "Ah, no. That's the way they come. Ain't none of 'em got a stitch of paper."

Disappointed yet hopeful, Bessie thoroughly inspected the best of the bunch. She felt like a test pilot again, taking up a suspect aircraft. Bessie made a few mechanical tweaks with Vernon's assistance until she felt confident of the plane's airworthiness. Moments later, she was in the air and back on the ground safely after a very short flight. The JN-4 engine sputtered, then quieted to a stop as Bessie climbed out of the cockpit, inspecting the engine compartment with practiced ease. Vernon lingered at the wingtip, watching her closely.

"Nothing hangin', nothing drippin'?" he asked, his tone both a question and a statement of dismissal.

Bessie took a last, decisive look at the engine and let a hint of a smile cross her face. "Guess not," she replied, folding her arms. "Now, how much you asking for these hundred-dollar airplanes?"

Vernon crossed his arms, scoffing. "Ain't no bargaining. Four hundred cash," he said, unmoved. "Tank of gas, bill of sale. Take it or leave it."

Bessie frowned, then nodded slightly. It wasn't the best aircraft, but it was a start. She handed over the money and climbed into the JN-4 for another takeoff. This time, dust clouds arose as Bessie advanced the throttle, and the aircraft accelerated. She gratefully reached three hundred feet when she noticed the sound of the engine changing. Bessie felt a loss of power, and her test pilot instincts kicked in. Trailing heavy black smoke, the aircraft pitched downward. Bessie knew there was no time to panic. Her eyes focused intensely on the ground to find the safest place to land. The fields grew closer each second as the reality of her situation sank in. She would have to land, and it was going to be a rough one.

CHAPTER FIFTEEN

Aftermath

I n the hospital room, shafts of sunlight poured through slatted blinds, casting pale bars across the stark white walls. The antiseptic scent of disinfectant hung heavy in the air, blending with the faint aroma of gauze and iodine. Bessie lay on the stiff hospital bed, her face a patchwork of bruises beneath the bandages that framed her head. A heavy plaster cast enclosed her left leg, immobilizing it from hip to ankle. She stirred, her eyelids fluttering in the dappled light.

Susan sat close by, shoulders stiff with worry as she thumbed through the newspaper, its bold black headline glaring back at her: "Colored Aviatrix Escapes Death." The creases in her forehead deepened as she read, and when Bessie's eyelids finally opened, Susan's hands trembled, letting the paper slip to the floor.

"Nurse! Nurse!" Susan called urgently. "Oh, Bessie, my child!"

Bessie's gaze drifted, clouded, struggling to focus. She tried to rise, only for a sharp bolt of pain to knock her back against the bed.

"Momma... Momma?" Her voice was a fragile whisper, colored by disorientation and pain.

Susan leaned in, soothing but firm. "You're gonna be alright. Just lie down, Bessie. You've been through a lot."

"Momma? How? What… happened?"

Susan smoothed her hand over Bessie's, the softness of her touch hiding the steel beneath. "Just lie back, honey. You're in the hospital. Crashed your plane. You remember that?"

Recognition lit Bessie's eyes, followed immediately by the raw memory of impact, the flash of blinding pain. She inhaled sharply, wincing as her body protested. "Oh, my plane," she murmured, teeth gritted. "Damn, it hurts, Momma."

The door creaked open, and a young nurse stepped inside. Her starched white uniform was pristine, and her posture exuded quiet confidence. With a quick nod, she took in Bessie's stirring.

"Hold on, don't go nowhere," she said, an easy warmth in her voice as she took one more look at Bessie. "I'm gonna get the doctor."

As the nurse slipped back into the hallway, Bessie gave a wry chuckle despite the pain. "I hope the heck she's talking to you, Momma, 'cause I don't think I'm going anywhere too fast."

Bessie knew she was lucky to be alive, but she was also impatient with her recovery. When she was finally well enough to leave the hospital, she did so on crutches and returned with Susan to her Chicago apartment to recuperate. As she half-reclined on the couch in a room scented from the well-wishing bouquets that decorated the apartment in vases, she wondered if, when, and how she would ever return to flying.

A day later, there was a knock on the door, and Susan moved to open it. Three visitors stepped through the doorway, each bringing a smile to Bessie's face.

Robert entered first, holding a bouquet of roses and a warm smile. "'Gather ye rosebuds while ye may,'" he said, quoting softly, "Old time is still a-flying." David and Jessie followed him in.

Bessie's spirit was undimmed by the physical pain that lurked beneath. "Well, I'm glad one of us is still flying," she said. She futilely attempted to reach for the bouquet, but Susan intervened, gracefully intercepting the flowers.

"Lemme put those in some water," Susan said in her motherly and brisk tone. "Gentlemen, make yourselves comfortable."

She waved the men into the room, noting they were short of on chairs. With a quick, efficient movement, Susan disappeared into the kitchen and returned, setting an extra chair down for David and Jessie before sitting beside Bessie at the end of the couch.

Robert was a blend of casual confidence and quiet admiration. "So, how is the patient today?"

"Fair to middling," Bessie replied, her tone laced with a familiar resilience.

Susan chuckled, a glint of pride flashing in her eyes. "And that's from a girl who knows a bit about cotton."

The group laughed, sharing the warmth of easy camaraderie. Bessie shifted slightly on the couch, a hint of discomfort crossing her face. "The doctor took the top half of the cast off yesterday," she said. "Ribs are healed, but they're still tender."

Jessie, who had been quietly observing from the edge of his seat, nodded in sympathy. "How's the rest of the leg doing?"

"A little sore," she admitted, with a trace of irritation at the constraints her body imposed. "Itches a bit." Her expression grew determined, her gaze shifting to David. "Now, I appreciate y'all coming to see me, but let's get down to it. David, when can you book me another show?"

David held up his hands, cautioning her with a shake of his head. "Whoa up there, Bess. I can't book anything until I see you walking on that post of yours. How much longer does the doctor say that's gonna be?"

Bessie rolled her eyes, her voice insistent. "Just a few more weeks."

Beside her, Susan's brow furrowed, a faint frown tugging at her mouth. "More like two months," she corrected, her tone blunt.

"Momma!" Bessie protested, a mix of exasperation and affection in her voice.

"That's the truth of it," Susan replied firmly, crossing her arms. "You don't want no booking you can't make. Them folks in Santa Monica weren't too happy when you didn't show up."

Bessie settled deeper into the couch. "People are always going to talk. Good or bad. The question is, do we know who we are?" She gestured to the plaster cast that held her leg captive. "Besides, I think I had a decent excuse."

Susan's face softened, a glimmer of pride shining through. "Oh, you did, child, but they didn't know about that 'til the next day's papers. Promoter wasn't too happy, neither."

Robert nodded in agreement. His tone was gentle yet firm. "When you get out on the road, you'll have to give it your all, Bess. There'll be time once you've healed."

Bessie's jaw tightened and her eyes flashed fiercely. "David, I want to play in the South. I want to fly in Houston, Dallas…" She hesitated, then added with a stubborn chin lift, "Heck, I want to fly Waxahachie. And Birmingham."

David's expression grew troubled, his voice dropping to a cautious tone. "I don't think that's a good idea, Bess. They aren't ready yet."

Her eyes were hard, and her voice was low and unyielding. "David, when I get rid of this anchor, it's ready or not—here I come. I haven't traveled this far to stop now."

David held her gaze, his expression conflicted. "Bessie,

things aren't a whole lot better than when you left Texas. You know what happened in Tulsa."

"It doesn't matter," she answered in a matter-of-fact tone, knowing he was referring to the attack on the primarily black Greenwood District in Oklahoma's big city. "You book me, or I'll find someone who will."

David's eyes softened, but his reluctance was evident. "Bessie, it's not safe."

"David, I want a fly'n school with every fiber of my being, but I've got to show my people we can move forward. Can't do that if I'm hiding up north."

David looked at Robert and Jessie for support, but they both avoided direct eye contact. "Sorry, Bess. If I book you in a show and you get hurt flying, I can accept that. It's part of the deal. If I put you in the way of harm when I know things aren't safe, that's another matter."

She smiled, a hint of affection mingling with her frustration. "David, I love you. I understand you're concerned, but don't worry about me. Every day, I'm moving closer to my goal."

CHAPTER SIXTEEN

Leading the Way

M onths later, Bessie felt completely recovered, and David grew tired of her insistent requests to perform air shows in the South. Finally, he relented to Bessie's request to arrange an air show in her hometown of Waxahachie.

A day before the show, she taxied onto the fairgrounds she knew so well. The familiar landscape was draped in a warm glow from the late afternoon sun with its faded wooden structures and colorful tents dotting the grounds. She thought of the people of Waxahachie and how much she wanted to give them a good show. She maneuvered the plane about fifty yards from a small, white-washed building beside the towering bleachers, its green shutters framing the windows. The sign on the roof proclaimed "Exposition Office" in bold letters as an invitation and a deterrent. Cars, gleaming relics of the past, parked haphazardly around the office, their owners busy with preparations for the day's festivities.

As she climbed out of the airplane, she saw Reverend Miller come into view. A broad smile spread across his face as he approached her. The sun glinted off his Model T parked nearby.

"I thank the Lord you lived through that crash in California," Reverend Miller exclaimed, his voice booming with genuine relief and embracing her warmly. "We read it in the papers. Had the whole congregation praying for you."

Bessie smiled, her gaze drifting towards the horizon where

her hometown nestled in the distance. "Well, Reverend Miller it must have worked, because here I am. Is everyone as excited as I am?"

Miller's expression shifted, a shadow flickering across his features. "Well, we were, but some things have come up. I mean, things haven't changed as much as you might imagine. As much as we'd like."

Bessie's brow furrowed. "By that, you mean?"

"They ain't going to let people of the race attend. We have to stay outside the fence."

A fire ignited within her. The indignation coursed through her veins, but she maintained her composure.

"Who do I have to speak to about this?" she asked calmly.

Reverend Miller nodded toward the office. "That'd be Mr. Finley up ahead there."

With purposeful strides, Bessie approached the office door, Reverend Miller lingering behind. Ellington Finley, a portly man clad in crisp white pants and a matching shirt, leaned against the doorway. His red suspenders stood out against the starkness of his attire. His flushed face showed surprise and irritation as he regarded Bessie.

"Miss Bessie, I presume," he said, his tone dripping with condescension.

"Good morning, Mr. Finley, is it? And it's Miss Coleman, actually."

"I'm sorry. Miss Coleman, then. Are you all ready for your big show tomorrow?"

Bessie's eyes narrowed, determination sharpening her voice. "Well, that all depends. The good reverend here told me an ugly rumor that people of color aren't invited to the party. Is that true?"

Finley's discomfort was palpable, like a tightrope walker swaying on the edge. "Now, Miss Coleman, you know how things are around here. There are rules."

"Rules, indeed." She took a step closer, her voice low but firm. "I grew up with a rule—the golden rule. How 'bout you?"

"Well, of course," he replied, a flicker of unease crossing his face.

"Well, good. I learned two versions of the golden rule. One is what the Bible says, and the other is that the people with the gold make the rules."

Finley shifted, glancing around as if seeking an escape from the mounting tension.

"Now I look around, and I imagine it took a fair amount of money to put up all those seats, banners and all," she continued, her gaze unwavering.

Finley nodded, albeit reluctantly. "More than a few dollars, yes."

"Okay, then. Let's discuss color. The way I see it, as much as you and your friends don't seem to like brown and black, you certainly do like green."

"I don't see where this is going," he replied, his voice thick with skepticism.

"Just follow along. Here's the deal. You either open the doors to everyone and collect a whole bunch more green, or there won't be a show."

Finley's expression morphed into shock. He looked around as if expecting witnesses to appear from the shadows. "You'd do that? Leave everyone hanging?"

Bessie couldn't suppress a smile, though her expression remained serious. "I don't think that 'hanging' is a good term to use with a colored girl from Waxahachie, but yes."

Overhearing their exchange, Reverend Miller stifled a laugh, his shoulders shaking as he turned away.

"I got enough gas to make Dallas, so take all the time you need to decide, but give me your answer in the next five minutes." Bessie turned toward her plane, glancing at her wristwatch. "I'll be right over there by my plane waitin'."

Frustration etched deep lines on Finley's face. "All right, all right. Can't believe this, but you win."

Bessie stopped in her tracks, turning back to face him. "And?"

"And what?" he shot back, agitated.

"And no separate entrances. Everybody comes in through the same gate. Sit anywhere they want."

"Miss Coleman, there are rules," Finley pressed, slightly raising his voice.

"Not tomorrow, there ain't," Bessie answered with an ominous finality.

Defeated, Finley sighed, and his proud posture changed to resignation. He wrung his hands, his agitation morphing into resignation. "All right! All right! Damn it. Doors will be wide open. Don't know how I'm gonna explain this."

As Bessie walked away, she said, "Simple, Mr. Finley. Tell 'em you were just following the golden rule."

The next day, the festive atmosphere transformed Waxahachie Fairgrounds into an energy field of excitement and anticipation. The vibrant sound of a marching band pierced the air as they paraded in front of the bleachers. Puzzled expressions crossed their faces as they realized they were playing for an integrated crowd.

Bessie's heart raced as she took to the sky, the engine's roar drowning out the world below. She maneuvered the plane with the skill of a master, diving gracefully toward the cotton fields surrounding the fairgrounds. The sight of the white blossoms bursting forth from the earth filled her with gratitude and pride for how far she had come. She felt the wind whip through her hair, reminding her of her journey and the battles she had fought. The ground rushed beneath her as she skillfully executed a series of daring rolls and loops, eliciting gasps of astonishment from the audience below. Bessie performed each maneuver for the Waxahachie people, who had been given dignity in the stands that day. Every roll and dive declared that she would not be confined by the color of her skin.

As she landed, the crowd erupted in applause, a wave of appreciation rushing over her like a warm embrace. Ellington Finley stood amongst them, his face lit with admiration and disbelief. Reverend Miller clapped enthusiastically with a broad smile as he surveyed the crowd—integrated, united in joy.

The following day, Bessie made her way to the Waxahachie schoolhouse with Reverend Miller at her side. The building was older but still a bastion of learning, standing tall against the brilliant blue sky. Bright and free children's laughter spilled from the open windows as they approached. Reverend Miller parked the Model T, and Bessie's heart swelled with anticipation as she mounted the steps. She saw some children eagerly press their noses against the glass for a better view.

Bessie entered the schoolhouse, her smile radiant as she greeted the students. They surrounded her, their faces lit with curiosity and admiration. She embraced Mrs. Braden, the warmth of their connection enveloping her. Mrs. Braden was older but still had the energy of a younger woman.

"Children, places, please!" Mrs. Braden called out, her voice cutting through the buzz of excitement as she took her place in front of the room. "Well, as we all know, we had quite a bit of excitement this weekend, didn't we? Well, this morning, we have a very, very special guest. As if she needs any introduction, children, allow me to introduce you to one of our most esteemed graduates, Miss Bessie Coleman."

"Good morning, children!" Bessie exclaimed in a melodic voice.

"Good morning, Miss Coleman!" the class replied in unison, their enthusiasm infectious.

"Well, well. It seems like a lifetime since I walked all those miles to this precious sanctuary," she said, her gaze sweeping over the familiar classroom. "But truth be told, it hasn't been all that long. What a wonderful journey it's been. Not an easy one, but who cares? Look where it's got us. So, who has a question for me?"

The hands shot up, eager to engage with their hero. Bessie pointed to a twelve-year-old girl named Patricia Rivers.

"Are you ever scared when you're flying?" Patricia asked, her eyes wide with wonder.

"No. I'm not scared because I'm very prepared and know what to do in all situations."

Bessie smiled at Patricia. "Let me ask you something. What makes you scared? Things you don't know or things you are losing control over, right?" Patricia nodded. "So what can you do about that?"

"You can learn things, and be careful," Patricia replied tentatively.

"Exactly," replied Bessie. "You go to school, you talk to people, you read books, you think. You get prepared. Then you use your mind to take you where you want to go."

Ten-year-old Caleb Smith raised his hand, and Bessie called on him. "My daddy said you done crashed once. What did that feel like?"

"It didn't feel any too good," Bessie replied dryly. "My engine quit, but I still had to land the plane. I had to make the best I could with what I had."

"But you crashed," Caleb countered innocently.

"Yup, I sure did. But it's what you do after you crash that matters. Do you dust yourself off and learn from it, or do you hide away and quit?"

A fourteen-year-old named Clarence Turner had patiently held his hand up for a while. Bessie nods toward him.

"What was the biggest thing in your way of learning to fly?" he asked.

Bessie smiled slightly. "Me," she said.

"How was that?"

"I had to overcome what I thought I couldn't do. Things people told me because I was a girl or because I was colored or poor. If you accept your limitations, sure enough, they're yours. The good thing is, you get to decide."

Several children nod slightly after internalizing the message.

"But here's the important thing," continued Bessie. "The earth and the sky don't care about your skin color. Man or woman, it's what's between your ears and in your heart that matters."

She could see by the expressions on their faces that the children were hearing something new and memorable.

The next day was Bessie's last show in Waxahachie. Reverend Miller walked towards Bessie's plane on empty fairgrounds as a few black workers picked up trash, disassembled bleachers, and loaded parts into the truck.

"Well, tell your momma we miss her when you see her next. When do you expect that'll be?"

"Might be a while," Bessie answered. "I'm booked on a speaking tour through Georgia and Florida. Gotta return this plane I borrowed. Then I'm off.

"Thank you for coming, Bessie," said Reverend Miller. "You made a difference in a lot of people's lives."

"I hope so," she grinned back at him.

PART 6

The Legacy

Father Clemens, Marion Coleman, Mayor Richard J. Daley, and Charles Horn at the renaming of a main road at O'Hare International Airport in Chicago in honor of Bessie

CHAPTER SIXTEEN

A Glimpse of the Future

———

Everywhere Bessie went in the South, the crowds of fans, reporters, and photographers greeted her warmly. In Atlanta, she packed theaters and auditoriums of primarily black people but many whites also. In Macon, she addressed an outdoor crowd at the Ebenezer Baptist Church. There were too many people to hold inside the church, so they met under an adjacent spreading shade tree where hundreds gathered to hear Bessie speak. The *Savannah Herald's* headline read, "Hero Aviatrix Mesmerizes Congregation with Oratory." Bessie enjoyed reaching people and inspiring others, but the constant travel and segregated railway coaches reminded her of all the work left to do. She sighed at the thought, hoping that all of her efforts were making a tiny ripple of change in the country's attitudes towards her race.

In Jacksonville, she met several pillars of the society for lunch, including Reverent Isaiah Cutter and Reverent Franklin Vetters and his wife, Deena. They were in charge of arranging her tour while in the city.

"I forgot to tell you we moved the venue for your address this evening," the Reverent Cutter said in his booming voice. "Tell her, Frank."

Reverend Vetters lowered his sandwich and lightly wiped his mouth with a napkin.

"We sold out the church. Had to move it to the Strand Theatre. They have an extra hundred seats," he said with a toss of his slicked-back hair.

"That's wonderful," replied Bessie.

"It's nice," Reverend Vetters continued "The theatre's got a brand new microphone, so you won't have to strain your voice. Also…," he paused for a bit, a charming smile creeping across his thirty-four-year-old face. "We had a board meeting of the Welfare League, and we're thinking of having an air exposition come May."

Reverend Cutter boomed into the conversation. "May first is the date. We'd be more than happy if the "Queen of the Skies," would perform."

Bessie laughed. "Her Majesty gladly accepts your invitation!"

"Parachute jump," Reverend Vetters said, politely truncating his thought so he could swallow his ham and cheese. Having done so, he continued comfortably. "Going to have one of those too. Local boy, uh.." He looked at Reverend Cutter to finish his thought.

"Melvin," he interjected, then realized he couldn't remember the last name. "Melvin….Melvin…

"Melvin Scott," Deena finished for him quietly, giving her husband a demure glance.

"That's right. Melvin Scott," Reverend Cutter continued. "Nice kid, but I don't know how smart he is, gonna be jumping out of an airplane."

"I'm without an airplane right now," Bessie admitted. "Truth of it is the only one I've owned tried to kill me, but I'll find something. Always do."

The clergy members looked at her in surprise, not knowing what to say. Bessie's attention returned to her salad while the gentlemen thought it best to change the subject to cover the awkward silence.

"So, where to next, Bessie?" Reverend Vetters finally said.

"Orlando," she replied. "Then back here to Jacksonville for the show, I guess."

****

It had been a tough year for Bessie. With her flying income at an all-time low, she had used some of her savings to rent a space and open the Sky High Beauty Parlor in Orlando as a back-up plan to flying. Now, her aviation dreams rested on the success of the upcoming Jacksonville show.

The Florida morning sun shone brightly on Bessie as if, attempting to lift her spirits with its rays as she walked into the Sky High. The air was thick with the familiar scent of nail polish and fragrant lotions which always transported Bessie back to her barber shop days in Chicago instantly.

Bessie seated herself at a manicure table across from Alice Hill, a woman in her forties of medium build, whose warm smile brought a sense of comfort to the otherwise bustling shop. She was Reverend Ezekiel Hill's wife and Bessie's trusted friend, who also gave a wonderful manicure. She had followed Bessie's tour religiously and was an understanding fan. After greeting each other warmly, Bessie settled back in her chair, a shadow crossing her features.

"Alice, this is getting to me," she confessed, her voice tinged with frustration.

"What's getting to you, honey?" Alice asked, looking up from filing Bessie's nails.

"Living in limbo." Bessie sighed, a weight of uncertainty pressing down on her. "I've done so much but have so much more to do. I don't know if I'm ever going to get there."

"You'll get there," Alice reassured her. Honestly, look at how far you've come."

Bessie nodded, absorbing the words. Her gaze drifted past the large windows, watching the world outside. The hustle of morning traffic moved like a slow current. Alice continued, her voice becoming increasingly animated.

"Look at all the shows you've done. And the parachute jumps!" Alice said, putting the file down and reaching for the nail polish. "Nobody does it like you. And you've got those shows in Jacksonville coming up in May."

"All true," Bessie acknowledged with her tone a mix of encouragement and sympathy. "But I still can't find a plane. Nobody will rent or loan me one. I just want to be there already."

"Frustrations aplenty and not deserved," Alice chimed in, her voice firm with belief in her friend's talents. She shook the bottle vigorously, then set it back down on the table, twisted it open, and removed the thickly colored pink brush of nail lacquer.

"I've been on speaking tours for almost two years now. It's adding up money-wise, but you know what doesn't add up?" Bessie asked as Alice began painting her nails.

"What's that?" Alice asked with genuine interest, but not looking up from her task.

"Why don't people of our race get up and get moving?" Bessie's voice rose slightly, a mixture of passion and despair. "I offered to teach flying in California. Twenty dollars down and four hundred paid out over two years."

"And?" Alice looked up at Bessie before moving to the next nail.

"Seven letters of inquiry, excited news stories, but not a cent in the door. Should've had the school going right there." Bessie's frustration hung in the air like a heavy fog. "Last Friday, Ezekiel and I went down to the pool hall," Bessie continued, shaking her head. "Lots of strong young men—interested in me, but not in improving themselves."

"Speaking of Ezekiel," Alice interjected, her eyes sparkling with mischief, "he says he's got someone for you to meet. A potential sponsor. But I gotta warn you he's loaded, but white."

They shared a chuckle, the tension of the conversation easing momentarily.

"That's all right," Bessie replied, a teasing lilt in her voice. "I've met the type before. Might be interesting."

That Saturday afternoon, Bessie, Alice, and her husband, the Reverend Ezekiel Hill, were going to meet the new sponsor in St. Petersburg. Edwin Beeman lived in a fine house on a tree-lined road, where the inviting verandas of neighboring houses stood like guardians of a simpler time.

"Here we are," Ezekiel said, a hint of pride in his tone, as the Model T carrying the women idled up beside the broad steps of the well-kept Victorian home. Edwin Beeman, a distinguished-looking though portly man in his mid-forties, greeted them at the door. He had a well-groomed mustache and goatee, which framed a face that bespoke authority and warmth.

"Reverend, Mrs. Hill, Miss Coleman, please do come in," Edwin invited, stepping aside to allow them entry.

The Beeman house décor reflected a blend of comfort and elegance. Ezekiel and Alice settled onto a plush tapestry couch while Bessie chose a nearby chair, its fabric soft against her skin. Edwin positioned himself opposite, an air of seriousness settling over the room as he reached for a large silver platter filled with steaming cups of coffee.

"Miss Coleman," he began, his voice steady and sincere, "I cannot tell you what an honor it is to meet you. I have followed your exploits as closely as the papers allow for some time."

Bessie offered a polite smile. "One should not always believe everything you read in the dailies, sir."

"Oh, the reports of your aerial exploits are indeed fascinating," he continued, his gaze intense. "But what you are doing for your people is astounding."

"I merely relayed what you mentioned in your correspondence a few months ago," Ezekiel turned to Bessie and said, his tone respectful.

Edwin leaned forward slightly, his hands folded, eyes fixed on Bessie. "I understand you are quite close to your goal, having worked earnestly for many years."

Bessie's heart raced with hope and apprehension. "Yes, sir. I'm close. Very close."

"But I understand you need a tool," Edwin continued, his voice taking a serious note. "An airplane to generate the last requisite funds to open your flying school."

"Indeed, sir." Bessie's voice dropped to a whisper, the gravity of her situation weighing heavily on her. "I've been trying to rent or borrow one for my next string of shows, but nobody is willing to rent to—well, to me."

"I completely understand." Edwin's tone softened as he leaned back slightly, his expression thoughtful. "So I am prepared to sponsor an aircraft for you."

As Bessie's mouth fell open in awe, Edwin continued.

I also understand that the Curtiss Southwestern Airplane and Motor Company of Dallas has just what is needed."

Still shocked by what he was saying, Bessie stammered slightly in her reply.

"Yes, sir, they certainly would have what I need."

Bessie looked to Ezekiel and Alice to affirm what was happening. They gently smiled and nodded.

"Well, then. I will have the funds wired to the company straight away. You'll only have to high tail it out to Dallas to fetch it back," Edwin finished casually.

Bessie's heart leaped at the unexpected generosity. "Sir, I don't think I'll ever be able to thank you enough, but I have to ask—why? Why me? Why this?"

Edwin exchanged a knowing glance with Ezekiel, who nodded in agreement before turning back to Bessie. "Why? Well, many people are raised in religion and ethics, yet when it comes to practicing, they fall short."

Bessie absorbed his words, nodding slightly.

"The only way for this country to move forward is for people to recognize each other's humanity," Edwin continued.

Ezekiel reached for his coffee, silently affirming the sentiment.

"Along comes aviation," Edwin added, his enthusiasm rising. "Flight—a magnificent revolution in mankind's experience. What unfathomable potential!"

The weight of his words settled in the room, drawing Bessie, Alice, and Ezekiel in as if they were part of an unspoken agreement.

"We will all ride its wings into the future. As you so eloquently put it, the earth and sky don't care about a person's sex, color, or tribe," Edwin said, fixing his gaze on Bessie's, the intensity of his belief evident. "You represent the way forward—a glimpse of the future of our society."

Marion Coleman at the commemoration ceremony for Bessie's postage stamp

Bessie Coleman postage stamp

"Discovering Bessie Coleman" documentary poster

Bessie Coleman Barbie Doll by Mattel

Gigi Coleman at the US Mint Bessie Coleman Quarter Commemoration

Gigi Coleman in her one-woman show outfit

An All-Stars student and instructor on a flight simulator

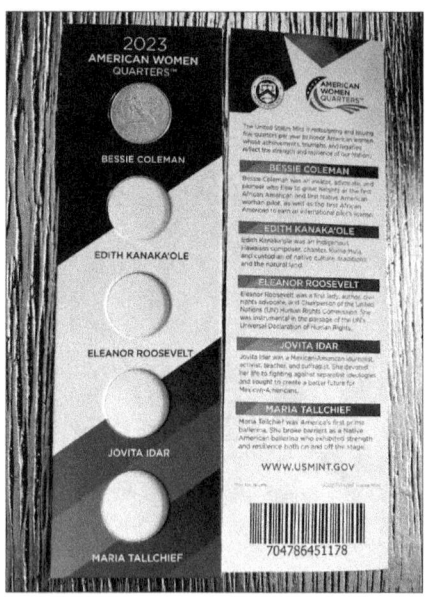

The 2023 American Women quarter collection folder (including Bessie Coleman) from the US Mint

Bessie Coleman All-Stars students pose for a photo on their fieldtrip to O'Hare

Bessie Coleman All-Stars students learn about aviation at O'Hare Airport

CHAPTER SEVENTEEN

Fateful Flight

———

A t the Curtiss Southwestern Airplane and Motor Company in Dallas, Texas, Bessie walked alongside John Hardwick, a man in his thirties with neatly combed brown hair. They approached a tired-looking JN-4 aircraft parked before a large hangar. The morning air was crisp, filled with the sounds of mechanics busy at work.

"Per Mr. Beeman's instructions, we've installed the newest engine we have in inventory," John explained as they drew closer. "She's been run up but not run in."

Bessie nodded, her gaze sharp as she assessed the aircraft. "That'll take a good fifty hours. Lifters will need adjustment about then," she replied confidently.

John raised an eyebrow, surprised by her knowledge of engines. "So, you might want to check the clearances once you get to Jacksonville. The rings will be seated by then for sure."

As they approached the plane, William D. Will, a thin mechanic with a grease-streaked face, emerged from beneath the cowling. He wiped his hands on a rag and extended a greasy palm to Bessie.

"Good morning, ma'am. William Will," he introduced, his tone friendly yet professional.

"Bessie Coleman. Nice to meet you," she replied, shaking his hand firmly.

"Pleasure's mine, ma'am. Well, she's not the best-looking bird, but I've been all through her," William said, gesturing toward the engine.

Bessie inspected the aircraft closely, her keen eye noting every detail. "Had a chance to take her around the patch?" she inquired.

"She was a little right-wing heavy, but I got most of that cranked out. Not perfect, but better than most," William answered, his pride in his work shining through.

John nodded towards the cockpit. "Want to try her on for size?"

"Let me check the gas and oil," Bessie replied, already climbing up the side to check the fuel level.

"They're good, just checked 'em," William reassured her.

"That's okay; they won't mind me checking them again," Bessie called back as she climbed into the cockpit, her heart racing excitedly.

After a few minutes of blissfully flying over Curtiss Field, the historic biplane touched down on the runway, its wheels skimming the earth before rolling to a stop with a soft thud in the warm Texas breeze. Bessie Coleman dismounted gracefully and walked back to John and William, who now admired her skill as a pilot as well as her mechanical sensibilities.

"What'cha think?" John asked.

Bessie wiped a bead of sweat from her brow, smiling broadly. "Engine's strong. Pretty much in rig. Nice job, Will."

William nodded. "Thanks. John here says Mr. Beeman wants it ferried out to Jacksonville. I'm up for that if you have no problem with it."

"I have absolutely no objection," she replied, the smile widening. "Better your sore butt than mine."

****

In Jacksonville, nightfall draped the Excelsior Hotel in an aura of elegance. Inside the bustling restaurant, the clinking of silverware and a soft murmur of conversation filled the air, wrapping around Bessie and her friends, Jessie and Robert. They were fortuitously in town for business and to catch her show. They settled at a corner table, the flickering candlelight dancing on their faces.

"Bessie, I saw that plane Mr. Will brought in this afternoon," Robert began, his tone serious.

Jessie leaned in, a teasing smirk curling his lips. "Not the healthiest horse I've ever seen."

"I know. But the engine's good," Bessie replied. "I want to recover the fuselage. Put 'Queen Bessie' right on the side, as big as I can."

Robert's brow furrowed, concern lacing his voice. "Bessie, he had two forced landings just getting the thing out here."

Bessie waved a dismissive hand. "That's kind of the way these things go. New engines need adjustment in the first few hours. Rest of it's rough, but she's sound enough."

Jessie's skepticism lingered, but he held his tongue. "I suppose you know best, but…"

"After I'm done scouting the drop area tomorrow, I'll take you up," Bessie promised, her enthusiasm palpable. "Show you Jacksonville like you've never seen it before."

As the dinner plates cleared, Robert and Jessie lingered over their coffee. The mood shifted to unease. Bessie excused herself from the table, and in her absence, the air crackled with tension between the two men.

"Don't like it, Jessie. Straight up, that plane looks like a steaming pile," Robert stated bluntly, unable to hide his disapproval.

Jessie nodded in agreement. "I agree. She knows it too, but if she gets this show under her belt, she'll have enough to fix it up, and it'll be the first bird in the flying school's flock."

William leaned back, studying his friend. "You going up with her tomorrow?"

Jessie cocked his head slightly, a playful smile dancing on his lips as he flagged down the waitress. "You want more coffee?"

The following day was the last day of April in 1926, the day before the first Jacksonville show in May. It was a glorious morning at Paxton Field. The runway seemed to glow beneath the sky, a vault of vivid blue stretching far above Jacksonville. A line of trees loomed to the west, their fresh green leaves brushing against a gentle breeze. Birds punctuated the air with song as they darted between branches, their small forms barely noticed against the endless sky.

The sundrenched hangars looked like a stage awaiting its actors. Robert drove a new touring car across the grassy expanse. The vehicle's tires crunched softly as he approached the row of hangars. Beside him sat William Will, his nerves barely concealed, while Jessie relaxed in the back seat, sipping from a thermos.

"I think she's probably in the hangar over there," William gestured toward the distant structure. He glanced at his wristwatch. "Must be. We're a little late."

The car slowed to a halt near an open hangar door. William Will stepped down from the running board, his eyes anxiously scanning the surroundings.

"Bessie, Bessie Coleman!" he called, his voice echoing slightly in the open space.

At the sound of his voice, Bessie turned, her expression brightening. She recognized that voice. He smiled back, his face alight with the excitement that always came with a day at the airfield. Bessie waved energetically to Robert and Jessie.

"See you later, up in the air!" Jessie yelled from the back of the car as Robert pulled away.

Will jogged over to her, a slight sheepishness to his stride. Bessie's stride was determined as she headed towards the JN-4 Jenny aircraft resting on the field's edge. The plane's metal glinted under the sun, showing the scars and stains of countless flights, each marked by the sun and wind that had brushed over its fabric wings. Bessie climbed into the back, fitting herself into the wooden seat as if she'd done it a hundred times.

The nose of the Jenny, the propeller, jutted outward, sturdy and slightly scarred, waiting for Will's hands to bring it into motion.

"Thought I was late. Sorry 'bout that," Will said.

"That's alright, Will." Her gaze lifted to the skies above, where only the faintest hints of clouds drifted like smudges on glass. "Looks like a nice day."

Will nodded toward the Jenny, a glint of pride in his eyes. "Gassed her up yesterday. Got the carburetor squared away," he said, his voice marked with satisfaction. "She'll give good power now. Bunch of crud in the bowl, but she's clean as a whistle."

"Good enough." Bessie's eyes sparkled as she shared a knowing look with him. "Looks like Melvin Scott doesn't want to do the parachute jump tomorrow. Need to go scout the field."

A hint of a smirk played on Will's face. "You gonna do the jump?"

She met his gaze, a slow grin spreading across her face, as bold as the day's sky. "Want somethin' done right, right?"

Will chuckled, hands stuffed into his pockets, his stance loose and ready. "I gotcha. You want me up front or back?"

Bessie considered it briefly, her eyes assessing the horizon beyond the Jenny. "Don't make any difference. Looks smooth enough. I'll just stand up when we get there."

Will strode to the front of the aircraft, hands gripping the propeller's upward-sloped blade. He braced himself, eyes narrowing with focus.

"Contact!"

The old Jenny trembled under Bessie's firm grip. Its canvas skin stretched taut against the wooden frame, and the faint scent of machine oil mingled with the aroma of wild grass. Bessie moved the magneto switch to "On."

"Contact!" Her voice rang out with authority, cutting through the early quiet.

Will gave her a quick nod, then lifted his leg, bracing himself before swinging the propeller through with a practiced, fluid motion. The engine sputtered to life, coughing, then settling into a low, rumbling purr as Bessie deftly coaxed it to a smooth idle. Each sound felt alive, as if the Jenny was eagerly awaiting permission to fly again.

Will tugged on the rope attached to the wheel chock, tossing it aside as he hustled to the aircraft's left side. The wooden wings stretched like open arms, impatient, calling to the sky. As he climbed into the forward cockpit, a small wrench slipped from his pocket, unnoticed, clattering faintly against the floor beside Bessie's seat. Bessie craned her neck around, her eyes sharp, a teasing smile on her face.

"You take her, Will," she called above the engine's hum, her tone half-command, half-challenge. "Go north. Watch my signals."

Will's smile mirrored hers, a mixture of excitement and trust as he eased the Jenny forward, feeling her come alive under his hands. The aircraft began to taxi, its wheels grumbling softly over the earth as they prepared for the lift.

The Jenny's engine roared, leaving the ground and climbing through the open sky. The earth slipped away and was replaced by blue infinity as Paxton Field shrank beneath them. Bessie's smile widened, watching the land drift into a patchwork of fields and tiny roads.

High above, the two exchanged silent signals. Bessie raised her hand, motioning for a turn. Will dipped a wing, leaning into the bank as they swooped in graceful ares, riding currents with a practiced grace. Bessie's head nodded approvingly, eyes glinting with pride as she watched him master each signal, feeling his quiet exhilaration mirror her own. Beneath the floorboards, the errant wrench had begun an uncharted path, shifting slowly with each turn, sliding under Will's seat, close to the aircraft's bellerank controls.

Now it was Bessie's turn.

The Jenny's nose tipped, and Bessie eased her into a series of wingovers, the world tilting then righting itself in a dance that brought them soaring, then dipping back to level. Gravity pulled and released in waves, the aircraft's frame straining as if alive, relishing the test of its endurance. Now wedged beneath Will's seat, the wrench inched closer to a critical lever, unseen, unnoticed.

Bessie took a deep breath, savoring the freedom that seemed to fill her lungs. She released the stick and shook it once — a signal to Will. In the forward seat, he lifted his hands, signaling his acknowledgment. He had control now.

Surveying the landscape, she unfastened her seatbelt, pushing herself upward to stand to see her parachute jump site. The air hummed around her, the slipstream clawing at her clothes as she scanned the fields far below.

And then, the moment changed.

A sudden bump, a lurch rippled through the Jenny like a violent shudder.

From the forward seat, Will's head whipped around, eyes wide as he saw Bessie's body drifting in open space, her arms outspread like a hawk soaring through the sky.

BESSIE COLEMAN

Epilogue

The news of Bessie's death sent shockwaves through the nation. Mourners of all races and creeds waited in long lines at three funerals to pay their respects to the Queen of the Skies. The first, in Jacksonville, drew five thousand mourners, a testament to her impact on the community. Images of Bethel Baptist Church overflowed with grieving faces, each one a thread in the tapestry of her story.

A funeral held in Orlando overflowed the small church, countless souls gathering to pay their respects. Finally, at the Pilgrim Baptist Church in Chicago, over ten thousand people attended, a staggering number reflecting her influence.

In 1929, the Bessie Coleman Aero Club opened in Los Angeles, a beacon of hope for aspiring aviators. Numerous opportunities in aviation for African Americans and women blossomed in the wake of Bessie's pioneering spirit. Josephine Baker, the renowned singer and resistance fighter, cited Bessie as her inspiration to learn to fly, a legacy of courage that spanned generations.

When FDR ordered the Army Air Corps to create a black aviation unit, the initial recruits came from the Coffey School of Aeronautics at Harlem Airport in Oak Lawn, Chicago. These aviators became known as the Tuskegee Airmen. They served with distinction as one of the most effective fighter units in WWII.

In 1934, William J. Powell said it best:

"Because of Bessie Coleman, we have overcome that which was much worse than racial barriers. We have overcome the barriers within ourselves and dared to dream."

Aviators and non-aviators will remember Bessie as a pilot of boundless energy, vibrant and full of life—smiling beside an airplane in her pilot's uniform, her spirit unyielded by the world's challenges. As "Queen of the Skies," she inspired others as she worked towards a dream. She also called our attention to the truth that the sky held for her and the many aviators of color who followed her, a final testament to her enduring legacy:

"The sky is the only place free of prejudice."

Beth Powell

ABOUT THE AUTHORS ⸺

Captain Beth Powell is a trailblazer in the aviation industry, a beacon of inspiration, and the founder of Queen B Production, LLC.

Beth currently flies as a Captain for the largest airline in the world and is known as an aviation thought leader, advocate, entrepreneur, and philanthropist. Beth's journey from a small parish in St. Mary, Jamaica, to making history is a testament to the power of dreams and perseverance.

Beth's mother dreamed of a brighter future for her daughters and instilled in them the value of education and the importance of a positive outlook. Beth soared beyond traditional expectations, obtaining her pilot licenses and a degree in professional aeronautics by her late teens. She was flying professionally by the age of 21. In honor of her mother, Beth mentors aspiring pilots and established a scholarship to mentor young aspirants in aviation, fueling the next generation of dreamers and achievers. In honor of Bessie Coleman, the first African American and Native American pilot, Captain Beth Powell led a historic all-Black female flight crew to commemorate the centennial of Bessie receiving her pilot's license.

Queen B Production LLC was born out of Beth's passion to share stories that impact and inspire, including the story of Bessie Coleman.

Her company's message is "Dream big and dream loud, then set your goal," and she produces content that moves, challenges, and celebrates the extraordinary potential within each of us.

Beth extends her influence beyond the skies as she serves on various organization's advisory boards and she is an also a member of various Aviation organizations. Her work with these groups underscores her commitment to in aviation and the arts.

Queen B Production LLC is more than a production company; it is a manifestation of Beth Powell's life-long commitment to empowering voices by sharing impactful stories, capturing the spirit of aviation, and igniting and uplifting the spirits of all.

Beth can be reached at info@queenbproduction.com.

Gigi Dolores Coleman

ABOUT THE AUTHORS ──────

Gigi Coleman is the great-niece of Bessie Coleman and is passionate about sharing her great-aunt's legacy as a trailblazer in aviation. Gigi continues the work of her mother, Marion Coleman, in informing the public about Bessie's achievements in aviation. Marion petitioned a postal stamp in her aunt's honor in addition to achieving other commemorations of Bessie's life. Marion petitioned a postal stamp in her aunt's honor in addition to achieving other commemorations of Bessie's life.

Gigi is retired after 25 years of service from the City of Chicago Water Management as an Assistant to the Commissioner. She also worked as a Senior Commodity Manager for Chicago Public School. She has since continued to inspire youth toward STEM education as a grammar and high school teacher. She also portrays Bessie's story as a one-woman show that challenges the minds of the young and old and encourages individuals to achieve their dreams.

Gigi designed a 501(c)3 program called "Bessie Coleman Aviation All-Stars" with a mission to expose disadvantaged youth to career opportunities in the field of aviation. The program enhances self-esteem and multicultural awareness, prepares youth for the job market, and supports educational and STEM programs. The program includes hands-on activities, speakers, and field trips to introduce youth to careers in aviation. Students learn about aviation history, experience flight simulators, fly drones, obtain drone certification, and even begin flight training. The program is affiliated with After School Matters at Gwendolyn Brooks Preparatory High School and was selected in its first year as the number one program on the South region of Chicago. The "All-Stars" have partnered with Operation Push Excel Stem Program for several summers and with the Archdiocese of Chicago, Chicago Public School, University of Minnesota, Children Rising in Oakland, California.

Nationwide, Gigi continues to work with agencies and organizations to expand her programs. Recently, she collaborated with the Oklahoma Department of Aerospace and Aerodynamics Commission.

Gigi holds a BA in Liberal Arts from Mundelein College, an MA in Sociology, and an ABA certification in paralegal studies from Roosevelt University.

Stephen Walton

ABOUT THE AUTHORS ————

Stephen (Steve) Walton is a retired airline Captain with a passion for grassroots general aviation and aviation history. Steve's interest in aviation was inspired by his earliest childhood memories of attending local airshows. During junior high, he would arrive early to school to read stacks of aviation magazine back issues in the library before classes began.

At sixteen, he combined his photography hobby with his love of aviation and traded a series of pictures for his first three flying lessons. The experience captivated him, and he focused on affording flight lessons by taking any job he could. Steve ultimately earned his private pilot license while his parents were residing out of state for continuing education. Having proven his dedication to aviation, Steve's parents backed his ambitions to attend Embry Riddle Aeronautical University. However, Steve preferred aerobatics to academics. He left the Daytona Beach campus for the northwest corner of Miami International Airport, where he took a series of freight jobs to acquire his Airline Transport Rating, Flight Engineer's license, and mechanic's license. He then finished his aviation degree at Embry Riddle with 63 credit hours of life experience.

Steve became Chief Pilot at a commuter airline, and then an upstart, before joining American Airlines. He was promoted to Captain in four years. As part of the volunteer search and rescue group, "Brothers to the Rescue," Steve flew one hundred missions, encompassing six hundred hours over a period of two years. He was involved in the rescue of five hundred souls in peril in the Straits of Florida who fled their native Cuba.

In 2022, Steve met Beth Powell, owner of Queen B Production, after an introduction from mutual friend Captain Linda Pauwels. Queen B wanted to make a movie of Bessie's life story. With his knowledge of aviation history and experience screenwriting for his son, who was attending a filmmaking school, Steve was an excellent candidate to write the screenplay. Beth and Steve immediately found joy and synergy in their friendship and interest in Bessie. After interviews with the Coleman family, Steve crafted the script for Queen of the Skies while collaborating with Beth to craft the story and develop Bessie's character. His script was used to develop the biography of the same name published in 2025.

Help Us Keep Bessie's Legacy Soaring!

Please connect with us to stay informed about new updates and happenings that celebrate the achievements of Bessie Coleman. We invite you to follow us on social media and visit one or more of our websites to stay updated.

Queen B Production LLC
www.queenbproduction.com

Follow along for additional aviation resources! We offer new aviation resources and inspirational content throughout the year!

Home | LadyAv8rBeth
www.ladyav8rbeth.com

 www.linkedin.com/in/Ladyav8rbeth
 https://www.instagram.com/ladyav8rbeth/
 https://www.tiktok.com/@ladyav8rbeth

www.ingramcontent.com/pod-product-compliance
Lightning Source LLC
Chambersburg PA
CBHW061747120626
46550CB00005B/1919

* 9 7 8 1 9 6 1 6 0 0 4 2 3 *